Punishment

This book expands the growing field of punishment ecology and advances an environmental theory of punishment that centralises Nature as a political force capable of exercising penal power.

In dialogue with post-humanist and new materialist thought, *Punishment* unsettles Western philosophy's casting of nature as a passive, inert backdrop to human action. Instead,it foregrounds a Nature that resists, recalibrates in response to, and co-produces social practice. This book asks what role this creative, responsive, more-than-human Nature plays in both the practice and lived experience of criminal punishment. Centring chemical and fungal agency, *Punishment* disrupts conventional legal narratives surrounding prisoner illness and the lethal injection, revealing how contemporary forms of penal power are entangled with the political economies of colonialism, racial capitalism, industrial agriculture, and resource extractivism. In bringing these entanglements into sharper focus, this book develops an ethics of punishment that moves beyond the individual and institutional frames of traditional sociolegal approaches to show how penal power is not only environmentally distributed but proliferates through material systems in ways that blur the spatial and temporal boundaries through which we typically organise the world and imagine our place within it.

This book will be a key text for criminologists, sociologists, jurists, and others interested in criminal law and penal theory.

Sabrina Gilani is Associate Professor in Law at the University of Sussex in Brighton, U.K.

Part of the NEW TRAJECTORIES IN LAW series

for information about the series and details of previous and forthcoming titles, see https://www.routledge.com/New-Trajectories-in-Law/book-series/NTL

A GlassHouse Book

Punishment

New Trajectories in Law

Sabrina Gilani

Routledge
Taylor & Francis Group
a GlassHouse Book

First published 2026
by Routledge
4 Park Square, Milton Park, Abingdon, Oxon OX14 4RN

and by Routledge
605 Third Avenue, New York, NY 10158

Routledge is an imprint of the Taylor & Francis Group, an informa business

A GlassHouse Book

British Library Cataloguing-in-Publication Data
A catalogue record for this book is available from the British Library

Library of Congress Cataloging-in-Publication Data
Names: Gilani, Sabrina author
Title: Punishment : new trajectories in law / Sabrina Gilani.
Description: 1. | New York : Routledge, 2026. | Series: New trajectories in law | Includes bibliographical references and index.
Identifiers: LCCN 2026005322 (print) | LCCN 2026005323 (ebook) | ISBN 9781032434889 hardback | ISBN 9781032434902 paperback | ISBN 9781003367567 ebook
Subjects: LCSH: Punishment–Law and legislation | Criminal law–Philosophy | Corrections | Environmental justice | Human ecology–Political aspects | Social ecology | LCGFT: Law materials
Classification: LCC K5103 .G544 2026 (print) | LCC K5103 (ebook)
LC record available at https://lccn.loc.gov/2026005322
LC ebook record available at https://lccn.loc.gov/2026005323

ISBN: 978-1-032-43488-9 (hbk)
ISBN: 978-1-032-43490-2 (pbk)
ISBN: 978-1-003-36756-7 (ebk)

DOI: 10.4324/9781003367567

Typeset in Times New Roman
by Deanta Global Publishing Services, Chennai, India

Contents

Introduction

This is a book about criminal punishment, how we punish, where we punish, and who (or what) are its objects or targets. The "how, where, whom" are important sociolegal questions because they essentially distinguish unlawful from legally justified forms of punishment, ethical from unethical punitive practice. A fundamental argument of this book is that existing sociolegal debates have narrowed the "how, where, and whom" questions to such an extent that consequential sites, structures and currents of power and affect remain neglected within these discussions. Much of the mainstream sociolegal discourse on criminal punishment focuses almost exclusively on institutional exercises of power and individual exercises of resistance. While these are certainly important, they do not tell the whole story. The state institutions and individuals at the centre of these narratives are themselves embedded in larger global and planetary flows of capital, matter, and agency that may be conditioned by social practice, but are also themselves forces that must be reckoned with.

Central to this idea that we are living in the "Anthropocene", a moment in geological time where human activity has been linked to a steady and increasing disruption of planetary life and a destabilisation of environmental forces,[1] is a rising awareness that the transcendental vision of human life which has become central to western thought simply cannot be sustained by the new revelations of science and technology. The Cartesian bifurcation of nature from culture, human from nonhuman, body from mind has all but "broken down" in the face of emerging trends that speak to a "deep intertwining of the fates of nature and humankind".[2] The Anthropocene necessitates a rethinking

1 Clive Hamilton, Christophe Bonneuil and Francois Gemenne, 'Thinking the Anthropocene' in *The Anthropocene and the Global Environmental Crisis: Rethinking Modernity in a New Epoch* (Routledge 2015) 1–13. Jan Zalasiewicz and others, 'The New World of the Anthropocene' (2010) 44 Environmental Science & Technology 2228.

2 Eva Lövbrand and others, 'Who Speaks for the Future of Earth? How Critical Social Science Can Extend the Conversation on the Anthropocene' (2015) 32 Global Environmental Change 211, 211.

DOI: 10.4324/9781003367567-1

of social phenomena to account for this steady infusion of nonhuman life into human matters and vice versa.

While originally the study of the Anthropocene was largely undertaken by scientists examining the large-scale environmental impacts of human activity – atmospheric chemists, climatologists, geologists – more recently, interest in the Anthropocene has also grown amongst those working in the social sciences and humanities.[3] Common to their work is the overarching claim that modernist philosophy and epistemology have long "naturalised" nature so that it has merely become an "external backdrop for the drama of human history".[4] Modern narratives thus promulgate an image of human societies as impervious to "material and energy cycles and unbound by the Earth's finiteness and metabolisms".[5]

But humans are material entities. As bodies living in a world, human survival and flourishing depend on that world. Perhaps no other moment in modern human history has exposed this interrelationality between humans and their environment more than the COVID pandemic, spanning the better parts of 2020 and 2021. The SARS-CoV-2 virus did not only infect human bodies but imposed itself into the most intimate areas of human social and political life. Its pathogenicity conditioned our exercise of governmental powers, the direction of our judicial rulings, the formulation of economic and public health policy, the crafting of foreign relations, and the forging of interpersonal relations between intimate partners.[6] Traces of its viral presence can still be found in bodies suffering from long-COVID syndrome, where the history of infection expresses itself in the form of a neurological condition that continues to affect the physical health, social routines, sense of self, and emotional well-being of sufferers on a daily basis.[7] Fragments of this relationship

3 Elizabeth Grosz, Kathryn Yusoff and Nigel Clark, 'An Interview with Elizabeth Grosz: Geopower, Inhumanism and the Biopolitical' (2017) 34 Theory, Culture & Society 129; Zalasiewicz and others (n 1); Paul Josef Crutzen, 'The Anthropocene: The Current Human-Dominated Geological Era' (2006) 18 Pontifical Academy of Sciences, Acta 199; Anna Grear, 'Deconstructing Anthropos: A Critical Legal Reflection on "Anthropocentric" Law and Anthropocene "Humanity"' (2015) 26 Law and Critique 225; Lövbrand and others (n 2).

4 Hamilton, Bonneuil and Gemenne (n 1) 4.

5 Ibid.

6 Usha Rana and Jayanathan Govender (eds), *Exploring the Consequences of the COVID Pandemic: Social, Cultural, Economic and Psychological Insights and Perspectives* (CRC Press 2022); Philipp Wassler and Chiara Talarico, 'Sociocultural Impacts of COVID-19: A Social Representations Perspective' (2021) 38 Tourism Management Perspectives 100813; Suborna Barua, 'Understanding Coronanomics: The Economic Implications of the Coronavirus (COVID-19) Pandemic' (Social Science Research Network, 1 April 2020) <https://papers.ssrn.com/abstract=3566477> accessed 9 November 2024; Kanika K Ahuja and Dhairya Khurana, 'Locked-Down Love: A Study of Intimate Relationships Before and After the COVID Lockdown' (2021) 70 Family Relations 1343.

7 Hannah E Davis and others, 'Long COVID: Major Findings, Mechanisms and Recommendations' (2023) 21 Nature Reviews Microbiology 133.

have even crossed over bodily-space and generational-time, manifesting in the form of maternal immunity and epigenetic transfer.[8] To mediate and contain the trans-corporeal and multiscalar effects of SARS-CoV-2, societies have had to pattern the virus' international and interspecies movements, grapple with its plasticity, and attune themselves to its many variants.[9] It is difficult to argue that the kind of humans we were in 2019 - physically, psychologically, politically and culturally - has not been significantly altered by our encounter with SARS-CoV-2. The COVID pandemic is but one example of how natural entities can drive adaptations in human physiology, emotion, behaviour, and political and social order.

Given these planetary effects, thinking in terms of the Anthropocene represents a "ground-breaking attempt to think together Earth processes, life, human enterprise and time into a totalising framework",[10] and which not only calls for a "rematerialisation" of our existing "understandings of economy and markets, of culture and society, of history and political regimes"[11] but also an acknowledgement of human beings' radical materiality; that above and beyond all else, human beings are physical *bodies* in a world that they "become with", and that world has significant implications for the norms we devise and live by.

What Environment, Whose Law?

The notion of the Anthropocene has also sparked new ways of thinking about legal theory and the practice of law, and not only of environmental law (by which I mean human law that regulates the environment), as one would expect.[12] Writing extensively on how the age of the Anthropocene compels a re-examination of the modern juridical subject as an exclusively or even principally "human" subject, Grear encourages us to think about the ways in which "law is complicit in ongoing forms of eco-violence, economic predation, and the unparalleled imposition of precarity on humans and nonhumans alike".[13]

8 Sarah CJ Jorgensen, Lisa Burry and Najla Tabbara, 'Role of Maternal COVID-19 Vaccination in Providing Immunological Protection to the Newborn' (2022) 42 Pharmacotherapy: The Journal of Human Pharmacology and Drug Therapy 58; Rwik Sen and others, 'Epigenetic Mechanisms Influencing COVID-19' (2021) 64 Genome 372.

9 Miriam N Lango, 'How Did We Get Here? Short History of COVID-19 and Other Coronavirus-Related Epidemics' (2020) 42 Head & Neck 1535; Ruchi Tiwari and others, 'COVID-19: Animals, Veterinary and Zoonotic Links' (2020) 40 Veterinary Quarterly 169.

10 Hamilton, Bonneuil and Gemenne (n 1) 2.

11 Ibid., 4.

12 Michelle Lim (ed), *Charting Environmental Law Futures in the Anthropocene* (Springer 2019); Louis J Kotze, *Environmental Law and Governance for the Anthropocene* (Hart Publishing 2017).

13 Anna Grear, 'Legal Imaginaries and the Anthropocene: 'Of' and "For"' (2020) 31 Law and Critique 351, 355.

But the Anthropocene forces us to question not only the trajectory of human law but the very idea that law-making is an exclusively human enterprise. The nonhuman world also demonstrates jurisgenerative potential. The critical environmental law that Philippopoulos-Mihalopoulos proposes urges us to think about environmental law "as more than the sum of its human parts"; environmental law has a "posthuman emergence",[14] requiring new conceptual frames of thought. Similarly, Davies argues that humans are part of a *nomos*, a normative universe constituted by a variety of things – animals, plants, rocks, minerals, microbes, viruses, seas – a Nature (with a capital "N") that, she argues, "produces its own values and norms".[15] This normative universe secretes a kind of "ecolaw" that jointly shapes the world by enabling and constraining its subjects and objects (human and nonhuman): "everything becomes subject and object within plural normative systems".[16]

This idea of nonhuman normativity has also been alluded to by vital materialists, who draw attention to how matter – food, metals, electrical grids, chemicals, viruses, coral – channels its forces across and through human bodies, imposing a kind of affective "thing-power" on human societies, and shaping human will, politics, and emotion.[17] In a sense, the idea of the Anthropocene promotes a new kind of political ecology of social phenomena. For Latour, there are two ways of engaging with this political ecology: "we can choose to engage in it *surreptitiously*, by *distinguishing* between questions of nature and questions of politics, or *explicitly*, by treating those two sets of questions as a single issue that arises for all *collectives* [emphasis in original]".[18] It is to this second kind of political ecology that I am drawn, one in which Nature is conceived as having power to influence the political economy of human relations, but also the opposite, human practice has a radical effect on the material shape that Nature takes.

This book sets out to examine how the natural environment – the minerals, rocks, salts, microbes, chemicals, climate, animals – constrains and

14 Andreas Philippopoulos-Mihalopoulos, 'Critical Environmental Law as Method in the Anthropocene' in Andreas Philippopoulos-Mihalopoulos and Victoria Brooks (eds), *Research Methods in Environmental Law: A Handbook* (Elgar 2017) 131.

15 Margaret Davies, *EcoLaw: Legality, Life, and the Normativity of Nature* (Taylor & Francis 2022) 1.

16 Ibid., 2.

17 Jane Bennett, 'The Force of Things: Steps toward an Ecology of Matter' (2004) 32 Political Theory 347; Stacy Alaimo, *Exposed* (University of Minnesota Press 2016); Stefanie R Fishel, *The Microbial State: Global Thriving and the Body Politic* (University of Minnesota Press 2017); Irus Braverman, 'The Law and Law of Corals: Breathing Meditations' in Andreas Philippopoulos-Mihalopoulos and Victoria Brooks (eds), *Research Methods in Environmental Law: A Handbook* (Elgar 2017); Andreas Philippopoulos-Mihalopoulos, 'Lively Agency: Life and Law in the Anthropocene' in Irus Braverman (ed), *Animals, Biopolitics, Law: Lively Legalities* (Routledge 2015).

18 Bruno Latour, *Politics of Nature: How to Bring the Sciences into Democracy* (Harvard University Press 2004) 1.

enables (and is itself constrained and enabled by) social phenomena, in our case, criminal punishment. It is the aim of *Punishment: New Trajectories in Law* to bring these normative worlds to bear on human law and decision-making, advancing an ecological theory of punishment that conceives of subjects and objects outside of the institutionalised and individualised parameters of modern sociolegal discourse. Such a theory of punishment takes as given the idea that human practice and experience are always situated within what is possible under, not only the political and economic conditions under which humans live, but also the biological, geological, and atmospheric constraints on human life. *Punishment* disrupts the conventional positivist conception of (human) law, as a set of rules devised to govern humans in their relationships to other humans and things, and adopts an elastic conception of law as a kind of legal normativity that is "emergent from interrelating things";[19] a *bio*law, a *geo*law, an *eco*law, a *chemo*law, a constellation of forces, "patterns, standards, directions" of doing things, that order human life and relationships by imposing their own values and "guides for action".[20] As the chapters that follow demonstrate, by following Nature's "lines of flight",[21] it is possible to uncover new and consequential (human and nonhuman) sites of power that warrant further consideration.

An ecolegal appreciation of criminal punishment requires, as Davies poignantly states, an attunement of legal theory to nature, to *things*, and to an emerging theory of science that challenges the mechanical laws and linear relationships of closed systems which emphasise "stability, order, uniformity, and equilibrium",[22] substituting it with modes of ordering that emphasise "constraints, invariances, constancies, regularities in our universe...*determinations* [instead of determin*ants*]".[23] What emerges then is a world of mystery and wonder, where "chance and necessity" are co-present "not with one subordinate to the other, but as full partners in a universe that is simultaneously organising and de-organising itself".[24] What might it mean to punish in such a world, a world in which the modes and effects of punishment, its intended targets, its hoped-for outcomes are responsive to nonhuman determinations? How does law manage these environmental interventions? How *should it* manage them? These are the kinds of questions with which this book grapples.

19 Davies (n 15) 2.

20 Ibid., 4.

21 Felix Guattari, *Lines of Flight: For Another World of Possibilities* (Andrew Goffey tr, Bloomsbury 2016).

22 Alvin Toffler, 'Foreward: Science and Change' in Ilya Prigogine and Isabelle Stengers *Order out of Chaos: Man's New Dialogue with Nature* (Verso Books 2017) xiv.

23 Ibid., xxii.

24 Ibid.

Setting the Course

Punishment's opening chapter begins by situating its ecological analysis within existing mainstream approaches to punishment. An obvious question here might be, why should environmental interventions matter to human law and ethical debates about criminal punishment? It is not as if plants, stones, chemicals, minerals, and microbes are capable of adhering or adapting to positive legal rules and rulings, and it is not that legal rules and rulings can change the course of nature. In this chapter I examine mainstream studies of punishment to show how the nature of human existence, *when* it is given any thought at all, remains rooted in a vision of reality that conceives of humans as discrete, autonomous, self-governing individuals, and the environment as the unresponsive setting for the theatrics of their affairs. Legal philosophy understands punishment using the figment of quasi-disembodiment, where space and time are fixed in the face of a universal conception of human nature. On the other hand, sociological and criminological approaches conceive of humans as beings embedded in sociocultural worlds which are crucial to the development of the individual self. While this second set of narratives considers the temporal and geographic dimensions of punishment, and may even extend its sights towards ecological critique, it proceeds using human frames of reference. For instance, it is only factors connected with the built, social, and perceptual environment, and not factors connected with the natural, and largely imperceptible environment, such as weather, chemicalisation, topography, microecology, or geological time, that capture analytical attention. The broader environment is largely marginalised as individual agency and meaning-making come to the fore. For this reason, I argue that mainstream studies of punishment (both its philosophical and sociological variants) are anthropocentric. Rooted in a modernist view of human existence, they often disregard nonhuman vitality and the complex material interdependencies between humans and their surroundings. Far from the passive and inert image we have of it, Nature possesses a kind of material plasticity, a capacity for agency, and undergoes processes of de- and re-configuring alongside its (human and nonhuman) denizens. It is only by attuning ourselves to the idea of humans as material entities that these human-nonhuman interrelations can be brought into sharper relief.

The second chapter of *Punishment* considers these questions of human materiality and material engagement by drawing on the insights of posthuman and new materialist philosophy in conjunction with science and technology studies. This chapter advances the argument that human materiality needs attending to, not only in terms of the body's perceptual capacities, but more radically in terms of its molecular, cellular, elemental, microbial, and chemical configurations. Bodies are sedimentations of interacting geo-, bio-, chemo-, and electrospheres. Human "being" is thus a fragile arrangement of these different enabling and constraining forces. Grosz uses the term "geopower" to describe a materiality-centred understanding of biopower that translates into "the powers of the body…understood as the powers that operate in and through living bodies, the powers of a body that can be harnessed for particular forms of action and passion".[25]

Geopower thus conceives of humans as connected with and continuously transformed by a Nature that is neither inert, nor calculable, nor value-free. This chapter examines how Enlightenment modernism's brute characterisation of natural and cultural worlds, as worlds *apart*, has been the subject of intense academic debate. It draws on momentous pieces of work that have, on the one hand, brought to light nature's latent potentialities,[26] its capacity to affect and be affected,[27] its creativity,[28] and its responsiveness to human activity,[29] and on the other, have demonstrated how human being has always been technologically-mediated,[30] materially altered,[31] and continuously affected by happenings in the world.[32] The environment is materially constitutive of human life; it is not only our social and cultural worlds that remain affected by changes in our environment, but our very *being*. Our molecular, electrochemical, and microbial makeup is in a permanent and consistent state of interrelation with the world around us. Human being is entangled with nonhuman being and, as Haraway notes, "who and whatever we are, we need to make-with – become-with, compose-with – the earth-bound".[33]

Taking this novel conception of human being as environmental artefact, the third and fourth chapters of this book examine imprisonment and the

25 Grosz, Yusoff and Clark (n 3) 134.

26 Bennett, 'The Force of Things: Steps toward an Ecology of Matter' (n 17); Alaimo (n 17).

27 Jane Bennett, *Vibrant Matter: A Political Ecology of Things* (Duke University Press 2010); Sara Ahmed, 'Happy Objects' in Melissa Gregg and Gregory J Seigworth (eds), *The Affect Theory Reader* (Duke University Press 2010).

28 Henri Bergson, *Creative Evolution* (Electric Book Company 2000); Latour (n 18).

29 Diana Coole and Samantha Frost (eds), *New Materialisms: Ontology, Agency and Politics* (Duke University Press 2010); Samantha Frost, *Biocultural Creatures* (Duke University Press 2016); Nancy Tuana, 'Viscous Porosity' in Stacy Alaimo and Susan Hekman (eds), *Material Feminism* (Indiana University Press 2008); Karen Barad, *Meeting the Universe Halfway: Quantum Physics and the Entanglement of Matter and Meaning* (Duke University Press 2007).

30 Donna Haraway, 'A Cyborg Manifesto: Science, Technology, and Socialist-Feminism in the Late 20th Century' in Joel Weiss, Jason Nolan, Peter Trifonas and Jeremy Hunsinger (eds.),*The International Handbook of Virtual Learning Environments* (Springer 2006); Katherine N Hayles, *How We Became Posthuman: Virtual Bodies in Cybernetics, Literature, and Informatics* (University of Chicago Press 2008).

31 Stacy Alaimo, *Bodily Natures: Science, Environment, and the Material Self* (Indiana University Press 2010); Samantha Frost, 'The Attentive Body: How the Indexicality of Epigenetic Processes Enriches Our Understanding of Embodied Subjectivity' (2020) 26 Body & Society 3.

32 Kathleen Stewart, 'Atmospheric Attunements' (2011) 29 Environment and Planning D: Society and Space 445.

33 Donna Haraway, 'Anthropocene, Capitalocene, Plantationocene, Chthulucene: Making Kin' (2015) 6 Environmental Humanities 159, 161.

death penalty in the United States, but by concentrating on its environmental agencies, the relationships between fungi, chemicals, weather events, animals, dust, rivers, and waterbeds. Chapter 3 investigates the emergence of Valley Fever within central California, a fungal disease that disproportionately affects prisoners, sometimes at a rate 1,000 times greater than the civilian population. Judicial narratives describe these disease-causing microbes as "naturally endemic" to specific areas of California, a fact that becomes material to determinations of legal responsibility. This chapter traces the history of this fungus in California. By studying its routes of travel, its patterns of behaviour, its environmental assemblages,[34] I explain how its presence within these epicentres of disease, and its movement beyond these borders, is connected with the political economies of human practice. Valley Fever is symptomatic of American expansionism, agro-industrialisation, and neoliberal capitalist practice, which promote overconsumption, overproduction, and environmental misuse. The disease's overrepresentation amongst prisoners reflects a punitive politics where the material effects of social inequality escape scrutiny in favour of a conception of imprisoned bodies as biologically vulnerable to infection and disease. Through their categorisation of Valley Fever into its so-called "natural" and "cultural" components, with the former being abandoned as scientific data that has no consequence for the law, the courts miss a crucial opportunity for identifying novel sites of power and continuing forms of sociocultural oppression.

Chapter 4 critiques the death penalty in America by examining the chemical interactions that bodies undergo during a lethal injection. Investigating the constitutional challenges that have arisen over the last decade, this chapter brings to light how justifications for the death penalty rely on a fragile "necro-chemistry" that presumes that the chemicals being used to cause death will interact with bodies, with the environment, and with other chemicals, in very specific (human-designed) ways and only under very specific (human-controlled) conditions. By drawing attention to the kinds of intra-activities chemicals engender and make possible, this chapter argues that failed executions are indicative of chemical agency and reveals how "humane" punishment is enacted through chemical connections and interrelations that are ecologically contingent. Chemical activity is influenced by a world of competing, conspiring, and cooperating agencies, human and nonhuman, and is driven by purposes that may, but also *may not*, coincide with human design

34 I borrow this term from Karen Barad's work. Intra-action refers to processes of co-constitution and mutual becoming. Whereas 'interaction' presupposes the prior existence of two independent entities that encounter one another, Barad argues the boundaries and agencies between two entities emerge as a result of their interaction with one another. Challenging the substance view of matter, Barad argues that things are ontologically unstable, always in the process of becoming anew as a result of the things, practices, and ideas they encounter. All matter is onto-epistemological or sociomaterial. See Barad (n 29).

and interests. Chemicals-in-nature generate their own norms, and these have significant implications for not only how societies punish but also *where* and *whom* they punish. Chapter 4 considers how the death penalty can be justified in the face of nonhuman agencies and intra-activities that may fly in the face of careful and deliberate human design. It asks its readers to consider the punitive dimensions of chemical relationships and, alongside this, the chemistry of punishment as ethical questions that need attending to in the age of the Anthropocene.

Collectively, Chapters 3 and 4 coalesce in a *materialisation* of law and politics that expose novel (human and nonhuman) sites of power and interaction, resistance and affect, jurisdiction and subjectivity, all of which deserve greater attention when debating the cruelty of imprisonment and the death penalty, and much of which evades sociolegal scrutiny at present. In particular, the book juxtaposes the "natural" discourse of soil microbes in Chapter 3 with the "synthetic" discourse of chemical compounds in Chapter 4. Together these two chapters explain how microbes and chemicals cannot be thought of as wholly natural or synthetic materials, but rather as socioecological processes-of-becoming that embody both human and nonhuman, living and non-living normativities. To treat these sources of calamity as either natural or synthetic is an oversimplification that, either "disenchants"[35] us by construing its catastrophic consequences as random and spontaneous, or generates a false sense of security that humans have everything "under control".

These substantive chapters of the book approach imprisonment and the death penalty using a posthuman methodology. Tracing the flow and paths of fungi and anaesthetics, in interrelation with a whole host of other human and nonhuman matter, forces, and politics, these two chapters steer the debates about cruel and unusual punishment in an entirely new and novel direction. Substituting the rights-based discourse of the past with a nature-conscious conception of agency and planetary responsibility, these two chapters set the groundwork for a concluding chapter that considers how an ecological theory of punishment contributes to the kind of ecolegal call for action Davies invites us to embody. In this final chapter, I consider how three of the critical insights developed over the course of this book – relational toxicity, trans-corporeal harm, and the productive potential of the pathological – can help us to reimagine the exercise of penal power in the Anthropocene.

Reading through these chapters, one can become easily caught up in a yearning for positive and conclusive evidence of a causal relationship between the things and events, human life and nonhuman processes that are central to its analyses. The image we have of science is that its grounds rest on the presentation of irrefutable proof in support of a speculative theory. Science,

35 Jane Bennett, *The Enchantment of Modern Life: Attachments, Crossings, and Ethics* (Princeton University Press 2001).

we have been taught, is measurable, exact, objective, indifferent. However, Stengers, Serres, Latour, and Whitehead, amongst many others, argue that the schism between science and culture is yet another example of the kind of "bifurcated reality" offered up by western philosophy and epistemology.[36] The desire for corroborating data is itself perpetuated by intellectual traditions that treat scientific knowledge as fact, rather than ways of knowing that are situated, cultural, and variable. This is often punctuated with declarations about how "only scientists should speak about science".[37] It is therefore my hope that these chapters are read as a kind of "framing" "of scientific knowledge", the use of "natural science as a 'thinking ground' for an approach to normativity in the living and the non-living",[38] and not as certain or absolute confirmations of cause-and-effect.

Punishment seeks to bring, amongst others, geological, climatological, microbiological, and biochemical worlds into deep conversation with human law and politics as they relate to debates about how, where, and whom we punish. It proceeds from the view that, as material beings, humans are dependent on the physical world, living and non-living, human and nonhuman, and for that very reason, conversations about punishment that remain confined to human intention and practice do not, *cannot*, give us a full account of the exercises of punitive power and normative interminglings that the practice and experience of punishment involves. The last thing that remains to be said is that the accounts I provide are also incomplete because they follow only certain material lines of flight and ignore others. Accordingly, there is still much to be said about the material relations of punishment, but it is my hope that this book not only ignites further conversation but that it is able to convince you that these are conversations worth having.

Works Cited

Ahmed S, 'Happy Objects' in Melissa Gregg and Gregory J Seigworth (eds), *The Affect Theory Reader* (Duke University Press 2010).

Ahuja KK and Khurana D, 'Locked-Down Love: A Study of Intimate Relationships Before and After the COVID Lockdown' (2021) 70 Family Relations 1343.

Alaimo S, *Bodily Natures: Science, Environment, and the Material Self* (Indiana University Press 2010).

Alaimo S, *Exposed* (University of Minnesota Press 2016).

36 Latour (n 18); Alfred North Whitehead, *The Concept of Nature* (Dover Publications 2004); Michel Serres, *Branches: A Philosophy of Time, Event and Advent* (Bloomsbury Academic 2020); Vicki Kirby, *What If Culture Was Nature All Along?* (Edinburgh University Press 2018); Barad (n 29).

37 Bruno Latour, *Pandora's Hope: Essays on the Reality of Science Studies* (Harvard University Press 1999) 17.

38 Davies (n 15) 10.

Barad K, *Meeting the Universe Halfway: Quantum Physics and the Entanglement of Matter and Meaning* (Duke University Press 2007).

Barua S, 'Understanding Coronanomics: The Economic Implications of the Coronavirus (COVID-19) Pandemic' (Social Science Research Network, 1 April 2020) <https://papers.ssrn.com/abstract=3566477> accessed 9 November 2024.

Bennett J, *The Enchantment of Modern Life: Attachments, Crossings, and Ethics* (Princeton University Press 2001).

Bennett J, 'The Force of Things: Steps toward an Ecology of Matter' (2004) 32 Political Theory 347.

Bennett J, *Vibrant Matter: A Political Ecology of Things* (Duke University Press 2010).

Bergson H, *Creative Evolution* (Electric Book Company 2000).

Braverman I, 'The Law and Law of Corals: Breathing Meditations' in Andreas Philippopoulos-Mihalopoulos and Victoria Brooks (eds), *Research Methods in Environmental Law: A Handbook* (Elgar 2017).

Coole D and Frost S (eds), *New Materialisms: Ontology, Agency and Politics* (Duke University Press 2010).

Crutzen PJ, 'The Anthropocene: The Current Human-Dominated Geological Era' (2006) 18 Pontifical Academy of Sciences, Acta 199.

Davies M, *EcoLaw: Legality, Life, and the Normativity of Nature* (Taylor & Francis 2022).

Davis, Hannah E. and others, 'Long COVID: Major Findings, Mechanisms and Recommendations' (2023) 21 Nature Reviews Microbiology 133.

Fishel SR, *The Microbial State: Global Thriving and the Body Politic* (University of Minnesota Press 2017).

Frost S, 'Biocultural Creatures', *Biocultural Creatures* (Duke University Press 2016).

Frost S, 'The Attentive Body: How the Indexicality of Epigenetic Processes Enriches Our Understanding of Embodied Subjectivity' (2020) 26 Body & Society 3.

Grear A, 'Deconstructing Anthropos: A Critical Legal Reflection on "Anthropocentric" Law and Anthropocene "Humanity"' (2015) 26 Law and Critique 225.

Grear A, 'Legal Imaginaries and the Anthropocene: 'Of' and "For"' (2020) 31 Law and Critique 351.

Grosz E, Yusoff K and Clark N, 'An Interview with Elizabeth Grosz: Geopower, Inhumanism and the Biopolitical' (2017) 34 Theory, Culture & Society 129.

Guattari F, *Lines of Flight: For Another World of Possibilities* (Andrew Goffey tr, Bloomsbury 2016).

Hamilton C, Bonneuil C and Gemenne F (eds), 'Thinking the Anthropocene' in *The Anthropocene and the Global Environmental Crisis: Rethinking Modernity in a New Epoch* (Routledge 2015).

Haraway D, 'A Cyborg Manifesto: Science, Technology, and Socialist-Feminism in the Late 20th Century' in *The International Handbook of Virtual Learning Environments* (Springer 2006).

Haraway D, 'Anthropocene, Capitalocene, Plantationocene, Chthulucene: Making Kin' (2015) 6 Environmental Humanities 159.

Hayles KN, *How We Became Posthuman: Virtual Bodies in Cybernetics, Literature, and Informatics* (University of Chicago Press 2008).

Jorgensen SCJ, Burry L and Tabbara N, 'Role of Maternal COVID-19 Vaccination in Providing Immunological Protection to the Newborn' (2022) 42 Pharmacotherapy: The Journal of Human Pharmacology and Drug Therapy 58.

Kirby V, *What If Culture Was Nature All Along?* (Edinburgh University Press 2018).
Kotze LJ, *Environmental Law and Governance for the Anthropocene* (Hart Publishing 2017).
Lango MN, 'How Did We Get Here? Short History of COVID-19 and Other Coronavirus-Related Epidemics' (2020) 42 Head & Neck 1535.
Latour B, *Pandora's Hope: Essays on the Reality of Science Studies* (Harvard University Press 1999).
Latour B, *Politics of Nature: How to Bring the Sciences into Democracy* (Harvard University Press 2004).
Lim M (ed), *Charting Environmental Law Futures in the Anthropocene* (Springer 2019).
Lövbrand E and others, 'Who Speaks for the Future of Earth? How Critical Social Science Can Extend the Conversation on the Anthropocene' (2015) 32 Global Environmental Change 211.
Philippopoulos-Mihalopoulos A, 'Critical Environmental Law as Method in the Anthropocene' in Andreas Philippopoulos-Mihalopoulos and Victoria Brooks (eds), *Research Methods in Environmental Law: A Handbook* (Elgar 2017). 131-155.
Philippopoulos-Mihalopoulos A, 'Lively Agency: Life and Law in the Anthropocene' in Irus Braverman (ed), *Animals, Biopolitics, Law: Lively Legalities* (Routledge 2015).
Rana U and Govender J (eds), *Exploring the Consequences of the COVID Pandemic: Social, Cultural, Economic and Psychological Insights and Perspectives* (CRC Press 2022).
Sen R and others, 'Epigenetic Mechanisms Influencing COVID-19' (2021) 64 Genome 372.
Serres M, *Branches: A Philosophy of Time, Event and Advent* (Bloomsbury Academic 2020).
Stewart K, 'Atmospheric Attunements' (2011) 29 Environment and Planning D: Society and Space 445.
Tiwari R and others, 'COVID-19: Animals, Veterinary and Zoonotic Links' (2020) 40 Veterinary Quarterly 169.
Toffler A, 'Foreward: Science and Change' in Ilya Prigogine and Isabelle Stengers *Out of Chaos: Man's New Dialogue with Nature* (Verso 2017).
Tuana N, 'Viscous Porosity' in Stacy Alaimo and Susan Hekman (eds), *Material Feminism* (Indiana University Press 2008).
Wassler P and Talarico C, 'Sociocultural Impacts of COVID-19: A Social Representations Perspective' (2021) 38 Tourism Management Perspectives 100813.
Whitehead AN, *The Concept of Nature* (Dover Publications 2004).
Zalasiewicz J and others, 'The New World of the Anthropocene' (2010) 44 Environmental Science & Technology 2228.

1 What Is Punishment?

Criminal punishment is a sordid affair. It appears to be a nearly universal social practice, though research suggests that societies do not all respond to harmful actions in the same way that modern state-based legal systems do.[1] Also interesting, given the direction of this book, it is not only humans that punish. Nonhuman animals and microorganisms also engage in sanction-like interactions as a way of maintaining social order.[2]

In western liberal thought, discussions of criminal punishment generally focus on two main areas. One is the philosophy of punishment, which examines the moral, ethical, and legal justifications for state-imposed punishment.[3] This field, rooted in legal theory, addresses the conceptual and normative questions that shape legal practice. A second group of narratives understands punishment as an institutional exercise of power and focuses on people's lived experience of it. Often referred to as the "sociology of punishment", this work spans multiple theoretical and methodological approaches. While the philosophy of punishment asks how punishment *ought* to work, the sociology of punishment interrogates its social origins, purposes, effects, and relationships to inequality and power to provide an empirical (and descriptive) analysis of how it actually operates in practice. Beyond sociology, this research also draws on interdisciplinary and empirical perspectives, including socio-legal, criminological, ecological, and epidemiological approaches to punishment. Collectively, this body of work has come to be known as the study of

1 Ada Pecos Melton, 'Indigenous Justice Systems and Tribal Society Indian Tribal Courts and Justice: A Symposium' (1995) 79 Judicature 126; Colin Miller, 'Banishment from within and Without: Analyzing Indigenous Sentencing under International Human Rights Standards' (2004) 80 North Dakota Law Review 253.

2 Nichola J Raihani, Alex Thornton and Redouan Bshary, 'Punishment and Cooperation in Nature' (2012) 27 Trends in Ecology & Evolution 288. Elisa T Granato, Thomas A Meiller-Legrand and Kevin R Foster, 'The Evolution and Ecology of Bacterial Warfare' (2019) 29 Current Biology R521.

3 David Garland, 'The Problem of the Body in Modern State Punishment' (2011) 78 Social Research 767.

DOI: 10.4324/9781003367567-2

"punishment and society",[4] and seeks to examine punishment scientifically through systematic data collection and analysis.

Despite their different aims, both sets of narratives centralise a particular notion of the "individual". Treating the body as a stable, impermeable container for the self, allows each to focus on the mind as the main site of meaning-making. Philosophical accounts, in particular, downplay the body altogether, offering a largely disembodied answer to the question "what is punishment?" By contrast, the sociology of punishment recognises the importance of embodied experience but still tends to frame the body as an instrument for engaging with the world and for expressing the inner self. Even accounts that emphasise the body's role in meaning-making focus mainly on body's perceptual capacities, , and how they condition individual encounters with the material and social conditions of punishment. Consequently, the *discursive body*, constituted through social meaning and value, is extensively theorised, while the biological body, presumed universal and self-evident, remains comparatively unexamined.

A further limitation of mainstream approaches to punishment is their broad blindness to Nature and its normative implications. In philosophical accounts, Nature – including the body – is treated as irrelevant because it is presumed to be governed by physical and biological laws and thus incapable of expressing moral values. In sociological accounts, when Nature does appear, it is cast as a passive, uncontested backdrop for human activity – a resource, a dumping ground, or a toxic environment – leaving the dominant mechanistic view of nature largely unquestioned.

Taken together, these blindspots in punishment scholarship reproduce a familiar western divide: a split between an animate social world controlled by humans and an inanimate natural world governed by mechanical laws.[5] This dualism has historically organised disciplinary boundaries in western thought using a series of divisions: nature/culture, body/mind, life/nonlife, biology/sociology, which help reinforce the idea of humans as the primary drivers of social life. . Yet, the world that we currently inhabit, with its extreme weather, rising seas, collapsing ecosystems, and shifting atmospheres, makes clear that human activity has never been the sole – or even primary – force shaping social life. Accordingly, interrogating punishment solely as an exercise of state power over rights-bearing bodies is therefore increasingly inadequate; it ignores consequential sites of power and forms of resistance. Punishment in the Anthropocene demands a rethinking of body-nature relations, revealing the profound and often neglected role of the natural world in shaping social life.

4 Jonathan Simon and Richard Sparks, *The SAGE Handbook of Punishment and Society* (SAGE 2012).
5 Alfred North Whitehead, *The Concept of Nature* (Dover Publications 2004) 30.

Justifying Punishment

In seeking to bring some much-needed clarity to the question "what is punishment?", Carvalho and Chamberlen bring together the many different ways in which people have thought about, debated, examined, and engaged with the idea of punishment. They discover that, even within "the relatively hermetic fields of academic research, different facets of punishment often seep into discussions, blurring definitional boundaries between description and justification, form and function, law and morality and so on". The study of punishment is "messy", theories and studies often overlap, and there is a whole politics around why some "aspects of punishment are made more visible, emphasised or simply naturalised as commonsensical, while others are isolated from specific discussions, invisibilised or repressed".[6] But punishment, being a particulary troubling use of state power over individuals, demands special justification. Ignoring what distinguishes it from other forms of coercion risks weakening both its legitimacy and the possibility of meaningful critique..[7] At the same time, it is quite obvious that the multiple and often competing narratives around punishment have great difficulty separating the conceptual definition of punishment from its justifications; "the question of what punishment *is* from what it is *for* is virtually impossible".[8]

When punishment is viewed primarily as an exercise of state power, its study becomes confined to a narrow set of concerns and a very specific set of actors. Differentiating punishment from other exercises of coercion depends on identifying the values it seeks to uphold and the purposes towards which its sanctions are directed. Different forms of punishment have been justified for their usefulness in protecting society from dangerous offenders,[9] restoring moral balance after the commission of a crime,[10] deterring wrongdoers and others from future criminality,[11] and/or holding offenders morally accountable to the community they have harmed.[12] These justifications rest on the idea that

6 Henrique Carvalho and Anastasia Chamberlen, Questioning Punishment (Routledge 2024) 14.

7 Lucia Zedner, 'Penal Subversions: When Is a Punishment Not Punishment, Who Decides and on What Grounds?' (2016) 20 Theoretical Criminology 3, 3.

8 Carvalho and Chamberlen (n 7) 13.

9 Norval Morris, 'Future of Imprisonment: Toward a Punitive Philosophy, The' (1973) 72 Michigan Law Review 1161.

10 Andrew von Hirsch, *Doing Justice: The Choice of Punishments* (Hill & Wang 1976).

11 Ernest Van Den Haag, 'On Deterrence and the Death Penalty' (1968) 78 Ethics 280.

12 RA Duff, *Punishment, Communication and Community* (Oxford University Press 2001); Antony Duff, *Trials and Punishments* (CUP Archive 1986); Joel Feinberg, 'The Expressive Function of Punishment' in Antony Duff and David Garland (eds), *A Reader on Punishment* (Oxford University Press 1994).

punishment differs from other acts of coercion because it is imposed by a body with legal authority, on an individual judged to have broken the law.[13]

As an exercise of state power, punishment becomes a rational enterprise of control. As Honderich explains, "[t]he problem of punishment arises in the first place because the practice includes what traditionally has been called suffering".[14] Thus, within most western liberal accounts of punishment, the state's imposition of suffering becomes legally or constitutionally problematic when it ceases to reflect the normative purposes for which punishment was justified.[15] Any suffering that is inflicted outside of these parameters can be many things – violence, torture, disease, politics – but *not* punishment. As Flew points out, setting the criteria according to which punishment can be distinguished from other kinds of action is crucial to "discussions of the ethics of punishment";[16] namely, we need to *know* what punishment *is*, its essential characteristics, in order to determine whether the forms we employ can be considered acceptable. At the same time, it is quite clear that the collection of works that comprise the philosophy of punishment does not simply speak about what punishment is, but also what it *should be*, and sometimes this draws attention away from the day-to-day processes by which punishment is enacted.

While the suffering body may indeed be "criminal punishment's most alarming cost",[17] it remains largely marginalised in western legal philosophy and practice. This is most apparent in constitutional challenges , where outcomes often hinge on judicial assessments of official intent.[18] Although many philosophical accounts treat intent as a normative concern, constitutional theory and moral philosophy offer conflicting views on how intentions shape the legal or moral permissibility of an act.[19] As Ristroph argues, while motive analysis may be central to attributing legal

13 Antony Flew, 'The Justification of Punishment' (1954) 29 Philosophy 291; Herbert LA Hart, 'The Presidential Address: Prolegomenon to the Principles of Punishment' (JSTOR 1959); Alice Ristroph, 'Respect and Resistance in Punishment Theory' (2009) 97 California Law Review 601. Ristroph identifies a similar understanding of punishment in her reading of Hobbesian philosophy.

14 Ted Honderich, *Punishment: The Supposed Justifications Revisited* (Pluto Press 2006) 4.

15 Michael S Moore, 'The Moral Worth of Retribution' in Ferdinand Schoeman (ed), *Responsibilty, Character, and the Emotions* (Cambridge University Press 2010); von Hirsch (n 11); Duff, *Trials and Punishments* (n 13); Antony Duff, *Answering for Crime* (Bloomsbury Publishing 2009); HLA Hart, 'Introduction' in John Gardner (ed), *Punishment and Responsibility: Essays in the Philosophy of Law* (Oxford University Press 2008).

16 Flew (n 14) 292.

17 John Gardner, 'Introduction' in HLA Hart and John Gardner (eds), *Punishment and Responsibility: Essays in the Philosophy of Law* (Oxford University Press 2008) xiv.

18 Alice Ristroph, 'State Intentions and the Law of Punishment' (2007) 98 J. Crim. L. & Criminology 1353, 1353.

19 Ibid.

responsibility, some punitive conditions are so inhumane that they demand legal condemnation, regardless of the state's intentions in imposing them.[20] The notion that legal intervention depends on establishing intent assumes that punitive processes are deliberately willed, and, more crucially, fully under the control of state officials and institutions. However, as the following chapters will show, while governments may design punitive processes to closely align with their normative concerns, punishment can unfold in unpredictable and unintended ways. There is a whole dark side of punishment that is marked by volatility and disorder, and which frequently escapes the bounds of human governance.

The body occupies an uneasy place in mainstream punishment discourse. While most forms of punishment impose limits on the body, the physical anchor of the self, the common view is that it is actually deprivation of liberty, and not bodily suffering, that is the target of contemporary penal regimes.[21] As a result, the body becomes absent or marginal in philosophical accounts of punishment, which often privilege abstract principles like autonomy and rights, over the lived realities of confinement.[22] This disembodied framing of contemporary penal practice also shapes judicial reasoning. For example, constitutional debates about the death penalty prioritise procedural efficiency and reliability over the embodied and emotional experience of execution.[23] A discourse driven by a turn to abstract rights and responsibilities gives us the impression that legal justifications of punishment have "no *need* for the body"[24] This idea persists even as penal institutions continue their systematic efforts to control the punished "body and its forces, their utility and their docility, their distribution and their submission",[25] and governments actively regulate punitive process to mute its aesthetic and emotional impact on the public.[26]

According to Garland, the philosophy of punishment "begins with a rather idealised one-dimensional image of punishment that treats the problem of

20 Ristroph (n 19); Sabrina Gilani, 'The Ethics of Capital Punishment and a Law of Affective Enchantment' (2023) 32 Social & Legal Studies 3; Sabrina Gilani, 'Sublime Executions and Material Affections: Law, Aesthetics and the Death Penalty' in Imogen Jones and Marc Trabsky (eds), *Routledge Handbook of Law and Death* (Routledge 2024).

21 Garland, 'The Problem of the Body in Modern State Punishment' (n 3) 767.

22 Ibid., 768.

23 Gilani, 'The Ethics of Capital Punishment and a Law of Affective Enchantment' (n 21).

24 Gilani, 'Sublime Executions and Material Affections: Law, Aesthetics and the Death Penalty' (n 21) 155.

25 Michel Foucault, *Discipline and Punish: The Birth of the Prison* (Alan Sheridan tr, Vintage Books 1977) 17.

26 Gilani, 'Sublime Executions and Material Affections: Law, Aesthetics and the Death Penalty' (n 21).

punishing as a variant of the classic liberal problem of how the state should relate to the individual".[27] As a result, he notes:

> conventional philosophy...has little of substance to say about the actual methods of punishment that is appropriate to use, about the nature of penal regimes, and the quality of penal institutions...If the philosophy of punishment often appears limited in its relevance and in its practical effect, this is because its basic conception of punishment has been shaped by the traditional patterns of liberal thought...rather than by close acquaintance with the characteristics of modern penal practice.[28]

In adopting an instrumental view of punishment, philosophical and legal discourse ignore the fact that "sometimes penal measures and institutions have social determinants that have little do with law and order".[29] As a result, the "law does not so much deny the (undeniable) bodily aspects of [punishment]. Instead, it treats them as beneath its notice, delegating them to the 'realm of prison administration' – a realm that is mostly unregulated by law and untheorized by sentencing theorists".[30] Nevertheless, as Garland explains, human beings are material entities, they exist in the world in embodied form, and "these bodies", and not just rights-bearing individuals, "are inevitably caught up in our practices of punishment, however much the law and state officials deny this intention".[31]

The dominant framing of punishment in legal and philosophical discourse is shaped by the largely unexamined assumption that punishment is inherently a function of the state – the only actor authorised to punish – against individual wrongdoers. This starting point not only constrains how punishment is conceptualised but also obscures the broader social, economic, institutional, and for our purposes, natural forces, through which punitive power operates beyond the state's formal boundaries. These frameworks prioritise abstract inquiries into the reasons and methods of punishment yet often fail to adequately theorise its social geography – *who* is punished and *where* punitive power is most intensely applied. Even when these frameworks engage with the more contentious dimensions of punishment, they tend to do so by relying on abstract concepts like moral blameworthiness and legal responsibility, rather than confronting the material and structural dimensions of punitive power.

27 David Garland, 'Penal Modernism and Postmodernism' in Thomas G Blomberg and Stanley Cohen (eds), *Punishment and Social Control* (Aldine de Gruyter 2003) 50.

28 Ibid.

29 David Garland, 'Sociological Perspectives on Punishment' (1991) 14 Crime and Justice 115, 117.

30 Garland, 'The Problem of the Body in Modern State Punishment' (n 3) 769.

31 Ibid., 768.

The Social Practice of Punishment

Moving beyond the narrow conception of punishment as state action against individual offenders, the sociology of punishment treats it as a socially embedded practice, and examines how the enforcement and distribution of punitive measures reflect and reinforce broader structural inequalities, including those of race, class, and gender. Quite apart from the measured, rational, and methodical image of punishment that emerges through its philosophical and legal conceptualisations, the sociology of punishment interprets punitive measures as instruments that shore up social norms and collective sentiment, while simultaneously reflecitn. Punishment is not a dispassionate and indifferent state-directed activity; it is frequently motivated by irrational desires and public demands for suffering.[32]

Accordingly, unlike most normative accounts, sociological studies of punishment are more interested in what punishment *is*, rather than what it ought to be. From this view, questions about how, why, and whom we punish are socially contingent. Punishment is not simply how governments maintain law and order in response to wrongdoing; it is also a tool of social control, frequently exercised by directing collective hostility towards specific, often marginalised, categories of offenders.[33] Consequently, sociological theorists argue that developing a normative theory of punishment is impossible because punishment "cannot be regarded as a general and universal truth".[34] Instead, understanding its causes, effects, and implications requires situating punitive processes within the specific history, political structures, and cultural context of each society,[35] interrogating how "structural narratives play out locally".[36]

By framing punishment as a social phenomenon, this body of work examines the effects that punitive processes have "beyond the population of criminals".[37] Consequently, although sociological analyses of punishment often start by focusing on the offender or institutional settings such as prisons, there is broad consensus that punitive power is dispersed and functions across

32 David Garland, 'Punishment and Social Solidarity' in Jonathan Simon and Richard Sparks (eds), *The SAGE Handbook of Punishment and Society* (SAGE 2012) 25.

33 Emile Durkheim, *The Division of Labour in Society* (George Simpson tr, Macmillan 1933) 86–95; Garland, 'Sociological Perspectives on Punishment' (n 30); Cassia Spohn, 'Race, Crime, and Punishment in the Twentieth and Twenty-First Centuries' (2015) 44 Crime and Justice 49; Henrique Carvalho and Anastasia Chamberlen, 'Why Punishment Pleases: Punitive Feelings in a World of Hostile Solidarity' (2018) 20 Punishment & Society 217; Randall G Shelden and Morghan Vélez Young, *Our Punitive Society: Race, Class, Gender, and Punishment in America, Second Edition* (Waveland Press 2020).

34 Didier Fassin and Christopher Kutz (eds), *The Will to Punish* (Oxford University Press 2018) 22.

35 Joshua Kleinfeld, 'Two Cultures of Punishment' (2016) 68 Stanford Law Review 933.

36 Ben Crewe, 'Inside the Belly of the Penal Beast: Understanding the Experience of Imprisonment' (2015) 4 International Journal for Crime, Justice and Social Democracy 50, 50.

37 Garland, 'Sociological Perspectives on Punishment' (n 30) 119.

multiple social layers.[38] This has produced studies of punishment that attempt to identify its social determinants by tracing patterns of historical change in penal policy, law, and practice,[39] examining the political and cultural technologies through which punishment is enacted,[40] and investigating how punishment is embodied and lived through the everyday experiences of individual offenders and other participants in the criminal justice system.[41]

The experience of punishment has been of particular interest to those who align themselves with the sub-discipline of criminology. While the sociology of punishment broadly positions society or culture as its area of study – criminologists probe the quantitative and qualitative measures of crime control and institutionalised punishment as a lived experience. Criminologists show a deep commitment to both centring and fleshing out the punished body – in all its perceptual and sensual glory– how it is used, how it is controlled, and the meanings it makes possible.[42] As Bruckert and Munn note, criminological texts are littered with bodies: "incarcerated bodies, stigmatised bodies,

38 Garland, 'Punishment and Social Solidarity' (n 33) 24.

39 Durkheim (n 34); Foucault (n 26); David Garland, *The Culture of Control: Crime and Social Order in Contemporary Society* (Oxford University Press 2001); Kleinfeld (n 36); David J Rothman, *The Discovery of the Asylum: Social Order and Disorder in the New Republic* (2nd edn, Routledge 2017); Dario Melossi and Massimo Pavarini, *The Prison and the Factory (40th Anniversary Edition): Origins of the Penitentiary System* (Springer 2018); Georg Rusche and Otto Kirchheimer, *Punishment and Social Structure* (Columbia University Press 2019).

40 George H Mead, 'The Psychology of Punitive Justice' (1918) 23 American Journal of Sociology 577; Austin Sarat, *When the State Kills: Capital Punishment and the American Condition* (Princeton University Press 2002); Erving Goffman, *Asylums: Essays on the Social Situation of Mental Patients and Other Inmates* (Aldine Transaction 2009); Katherine Beckett and Naomi Murakawa, 'Mapping the Shadow Carceral State: Toward an Institutionally Capacious Approach to Punishment' (2012) 16 Theoretical Criminology 221; Jonathan Simon, 'Punishment and the Political Technologies of the Body' in Richard Sparks and Jonathan Simon (eds), *The SAGE Handbook of Punishment and Society* (SAGE 2019); Jeremy Bentham, *The Panopticon Writings* (Verso Books 2020).

41 Ben Crewe, 'The Prisoner Society: Power, Adaptation, and Social Life in an English Prison' (2009) 89 Social Forces 3; Ben Crewe, 'Depth, Weight, Tightness: Revisiting the Pains of Imprisonment' (2011) 13 Punishment & Society 509; Mary Bosworth, *Engendering Resistance: Agency and Power in Women's Prisons* (Routledge 2016); Anastasia Chamberlen, *Embodying Punishment: Emotions, Identities and Lived Experiences in Women's Prisons* (Oxford University Press 2018).

42 Chamberlen (n 42); Anastasia Chamberlen, 'Changing Bodies, Ambivalent Identities, and Women's Punishment' (2017) 12 Feminist Criminology 125; Catrin Smith, 'Punishment and Pleasure: Women, Food and the Imprisoned Body' (2002) 50 The Sociological Review 197; Loïc Wacquant, 'The Body, the Ghetto and the Penal State' (2009) 32 Qualitative Sociology 101; Dominique Moran, 'Prisoner Reintegration and the Stigma of Prison Time Inscribed on the Body' (2012) 14 Punishment & Society 564; Dominique Moran, *Carceral Geography: The Spaces and Practices of Incarceration* (Ashgate 2015).

addicted bodies. Criminologists speak of gendered bodies, resisting bodies, and marginalised bodies. Bodies are *everywhere*".[43]

Despite its growing attentiveness to the body, traditional criminology remains entangled in western epistemology's commitment to scientific objectivity and is deeply invested in its notions of reason, rational discourse, and the ideal of a transcendental subject.[44] As a consequence of this, with few exceptions,[45] traditional criminology has "failed to attend to how 'lived bodies' are experienced across time and space as *sites* of social interaction".[46] To address this neglect, Bruckert and Munn undertake a particular framing of the body, not only as discursive artefact, but as "material object...They are not only *inscribed*, they are the interactive *medium* through which we negotiate, contest and experience the social world".[47] There is a dimension to punishment that is, as Chamberlen explains, "more often felt and lived rather than cognitively categorised and sociologically articulated".[48] Emerging fields like carceral geography and sensory criminology reveal how punishment inflicts harm not only through physical injury or emotional and psychological suffering, but also by exerting sensory and affective control, and fundamentally shaping what it feels like to be punished.[49] Herrity's work, for instance, explores how the prison's auditory landscape exerts pressure on inmates by conveying power relations and reinforcing hierarchies of control.[50]

Within these less conventional accounts, the punitive subject is not only embodied but exposed as deeply material, navigating its environment through

43 Chris Bruckert and Melissa Munn, 'Em-Bodying Criminology: (Ex-)Prisoners' Bodies in Time and Space' in Véronique Strimelle and Françoise Vanhamme (eds), *Droits et voix – Rights and Voices* (University of Ottawa Press 2010) 237.

44 Susanne Karstedt, 'Handle with Care: Emotions, Crime and Justice' in Susanne Karstedt, Ian Loader and Heather Strang (eds), *Emotions, Crime and Justice* (Bloomsbury Publishing 2014) 1.

45 Chamberlen (n 42); Heidi Rimke, 'Constituting Transgressive Interiorities: Nineteenth-Century Psychiatric Readings of Morally Mad Bodies' in Arturo Aldama (ed), *Violence and the Body: Race, Gender, and the State* (Indiana University Press 2003); Kate Herrity, Bethany E Schmidt and Jason Warr (eds), *Sensory Penalities: Exploring the Senses in Spaces of Punishment and Social Control* (Emerald Publishing 2021).

46 Bruckert and Munn (n 44) 237.

47 Ibid., 238.

48 Chamberlen (n 42) 8.

49 Bill McClanahan and Nigel South, '"All Knowledge Begins with the Senses": Towards a Sensory Criminology' (2020) 60 The British Journal of Criminology 3; Kate Herrity, 'Hearing behind the Door: The Cell as a Portal to Prison Life' in Jennifer Turner and Victoria Knight (eds) *The Prison Cell: Embodied and Everyday Spaces of Incarceration* (2020) 239; Alex R Colucci, 'Geographies of Capital Punishment: New Directions and Interventions' (2020) 14 Geography Compass e12548; Bhavya Gopinathan, Vaagdaa Vijayshankar and Sanghamitra Roy, 'Exploring the Relationship between the Built Environment of Prisons and the Mental Health of Inmates' (2024) 20 International Journal of Prison Health 360.

50 Katherine Z Herrity, 'Rhythms and Routines: Sounding Order in a Local Men's Prison Through Aural Ethnography' (Doctoral, University of Leicester 2019) <https://doi.org/10.25392/leicester.data.10310807.v1> accessed 20 November 2024.

an attunement to its sensory capabilities. But equally, this work alludes to the productive and affective power of objects – the "jingling" keys in Herrity's work, or the various implements of death in Colucci's – though it often speaks about it in anthropocentric terms, as the sociopolitical organisation or arrangement of space. A consequence of this is that the value and purpose of an object, for instance, the tools used to "inflict death" in Colucci's work, are always determined by turning to the meaning that is attached to it by the political institutions that sanction them, and the (human) agent who "wields them".[51] While objects are never treated as having a "life" of their own, these interrogations nevertheless make it possible to imagine punitive processes as multi-scalar phenomena. The punished body is perceived as nested within material networks.[52] In so doing, this work also challenges the inelasticity with which western epistemology has conventionally conceptualised time and space, as linear, seamless, and fixed units of existence.

The materiality of human existence is further foregrounded within the situated and affective ethics evoked by phenomenological accounts of penal control. From this view, human beings inhabit the world through their bodies, which provide a shared basis for certain forms of vulnerability inherent to biological existence. As a consequence, our physical presence, vulnerability, and capacity to feel pain are central to how we make ethical decisions and relate to others. While philosophical accounts of punishment typically ground ethical responsibility in notions of agency and autonomy – often justifying punishment through appeals to moral desert or social utility – phenomenological approaches conceive of responsibility as contextual and affective, arising from our embodied encounters and relational engagements with others.[53]

Penal processes and experiences are also increasingly being explored through interdisciplinary alliances that western thought has historically regarded as methodologically and philosophically incompatible. Biosocial criminology, for instance, examines the biological and physiological factors – genetics, hormones, and brain structure – influencing deviant and antisocial behaviour.[54] While there is considerable scholarly interest in the biological determinants of crime, far less attention has been paid to the biosocial

51 Colucci (n 50) 4–5.

52 Colucci (n 50); Moran, *Carceral Geography: The Spaces and Practices of Incarceration* (n 43); Hanneke Stuit, Jennifer Turner and Julienne Weegels, *Carceral Worlds: Legacies, Textures and Futures* (Bloomsbury Publishing Plc 2024).

53 Chamberlen (n 42); Shaun Gallagher, 'The Cruel and Unusual Phenomenology of Solitary Confinement' (2014) 5 Frontiers in Psychology 1.

54 Alan C Logan, Pragya Mishra and Susan L Prescott, 'The Legalome: Microbiology, Omics and Criminal Justice' (2025) 18 Microbial Biotechnology e70129; Worlanyo Eric Gato and others, 'Examining the Link between the Human Microbiome and Antisocial Behavior: Why Criminologists Should Care About Biochemistry, Too' (2018) 39 Deviant Behavior 1191; Anthony Walsh and Jonathan D Bolen, *The Neurobiology of Criminal Behavior: Gene-Brain-Culture Interaction* (Routledge 2016).

dynamics of punishment experience. Notable exceptions include studies that explore how incarceration interacts with biological vulnerability, particularly in relation to addiction, exposure to infectious disease, and chronic health conditions.[55] Some researchers have also identified a strong epigenetic link between incarceration and accelerated ageing, suggesting that the chronic stress and precarity of prison life can produce a "weathering effect" on the body's cellular structure, leaving prisoners biologically older than their chronological age. The heritability of epigenetic biomarkers raises a further ethical concern, suggesting that the harms of punishment may extend beyond the individual offender, potentially affecting future generations. Given the disproportionate rates of incarceration amongst racial minorities and economically marginalised populations, these biological harms are arguably borne most heavily by those already subject to structural disadvantage.[56] The image of the body that cuts across these biosocial accounts of punishment is plastic, environmentally porous, and biologically mutable. These studies bring to light an often-overlooked dimension of punishment – one that resists cognitive categorisation and operates beneath the threshold of individual conscious awareness. Its inquiries unsettle both the disembodied rational subject central to philosophical accounts and the embodied affective subject that underpins most sociological approaches.

These alliances between the objective world of matter and the subjective world of experience must also be celebrated for drawing our attention to the significance of immaterial forces, for how they position chemical changes in the brain, hormonal fluctuations in the body, and bacterial interactions between the body's microbiome as punitive forces that must be reckoned with.[57] These investigations, which form part of a growing interest in the ecology of punishment, give us an account of how the pains of punishment extend beyond, for instance, the formal limits of a prison sentence, and can now be thought of as unleashing forms of biological violence *within* the body, rather than just upon it. Although they do not attribute affective power or independent agency to these forces, they nonetheless gesture toward a nature-culture entanglement which marks their analyses as conceptually distinct.

55 Michael Massoglia, 'Incarceration as Exposure: The Prison, Infectious Disease, and Other Stress-Related Illnesses' (2008) 49 Journal of Health and Social Behavior 56; Stefan Timmermans and Jonathan Gabe, 'Introduction: Connecting Criminology and Sociology of Health and Illness' (2002) 24 Sociology of Health & Illness 501.

56 Mark T Berg and others, 'Losing Years Doing Time: Incarceration Exposure and Accelerated Biological Aging among African American Adults' (2021) 62 Journal of Health and Social Behavior 460.

57 Michaela Langmajerová and others, 'Gut Microbiome in Impulsively Violent Female Convicts' (2024) 84 Neuropsychobiology 1; Logan, Mishra and Prescott (n 55); Malcolm Coffman, 'The Neurological Imprint of Incarceration and Its Effect on Recidivism Notes' (2023) 37 Notre Dame Journal of Law, Ethics & Public Policy 251.

Giving Nature Its Due?

Admittedly, as an emerging field of inquiry, the ecology of punishment has taken punishment studies in novel directions. It has opened up otherwise invisible landscapes for analyses and exposed the plasticity of the spatiotemporal dimensions of punishment (and the bodies in them). It has even alluded to the human body's porosity to environmental conditions by spotlighting the intrusions of viral and bacterial critters and biochemical forces. All of this suggests that the ecology of punishment is well-positioned to consider what it means to punish in the Anthropocene, where the fragility of human existence is continuously tested by the volatilities of living in, alongside and through a dying planet. And indeed, researchers, particularly those aligned with the subfields of green criminology,[58] have responded positively to this mandate, examining how environmental hazards are shaping prison experience,[59] how our punishment practices are contributing to environmental degradation and destruction,[60] and how carceral infrastructures perpetuate environmental racism and injustice.[61] This research has also triggered wider calls for environmental justice activism. For instance, in the United States, the Prison Ecology Project has exposed how prison infrastructure – including buildings, HVAC systems, and waste sites – and institutional practices such as waste disposal, pesticide use, and power generation, are contributing to the rise of "toxic prisons", where drinking contaminated water, breathing polluted air, and consuming tainted food has become a routine part of the prison experience.[62]

58 Rob White and Diane Heckenberg, *Green Criminology: An Introduction to the Study of Environmental Harm* (Routledge 2014).

59 Taylor Carpenter, 'The Death Sentence That Is America's Toxic Prison' (2020) 17 Indiana Health Law Review 229; Mason Wilkes, 'Toxic Injuries and Toxic Prisons: The Legal Limitations of the Prison Litigation Reform Act Notes' (2024) 25 Rutgers Race & the Law Review [i]; Brenna Helppie-Schmieder, 'Toxic Confinement: Can the Eighth Amendment Protect Prisoners from Human-Made Environmental Health Hazards Notes and Comments' (2015) 110 Northwestern University Law Review 647; Andrea C Armstrong, 'Death Row Conditions through an Environmental Justice Lens' (2017) 70 Arkansas Law Review 203.

60 Elisa L Toman, 'Something in the Air: Toxic Pollution in and around U.S. Prisons' (2023) 25 Punishment & Society 867; Pierce Greenberg and Robert Todd Perdue, 'Prisons and Pollution: A Nationwide Analysis of Carceral Environmental Inequality' (2025) 72 Social Problems 783; Tara Opsal, Stephanie A Malin and Taylor Ellis, 'Prisons as Law-Violators and Sites of Environmental Injustice' (2023) 31 Critical Criminology 105; Tara Opsal and others, 'Layered Sites of Environmental Justice: Considering the Case of Prisons*'.

61 'Linking Environmental and Criminal Injustice: The Mining to Prison Pipeline in Central Appalachia | Environmental Justice' <https://www.liebertpub.com/doi/10.1089/env.2017.0027> accessed 11 September 2025; 'Prisons, Jails, and the Environment: Why Environmentalists Should Care About Mass Incarceration? – Dorceta E. Taylor, 2024' <https://journals.sagepub.com/doi/10.1177/00027642221142206> accessed 11 September 2025; Elizabeth A Bradshaw, 'Tombstone Towns and Toxic Prisons: Prison Ecology and the Necessity of an Anti-Prison Environmental Movement' (2018) 26 Critical Criminology 407.

62 Nation Inside: End Mass Incarceration, 'Prison Ecology Project' (2022) <https://nationinside.org/campaign/prison-ecology-project/> accessed 15 June 2024.

Given that prisons are often constructed in rural locations, situated in sparsely populated areas, and usually on lands that are in close proximity to industrial plants and waste disposal sites, these studies demonstrate how environmental burdens are disproportionately shouldered by inmates and prison personnel.[63]

Apart from their focus on toxic lands, social scientists have also endeavoured to include the natural environment by considering the effects of climate change on carceral practice and experience. Research conducted has shown that the environmental hazards intensified by climate change disproportionately affect incarcerated populations, how these infrastructures may "cross the threshold of cruel and unusual punishment",[64] and how existing legislative frameworks may be preventing inmates from seeking legal redress when faced with these harms.[65]

While ecological approaches to punishment and green criminology foreground systemic, structural, and environmental harms – rightly identifying ecosystems, nonhuman animals, and the planet as victims of toxic and pollutive human practices – they often remain tethered to legal frameworks for redress. Within western, state-based legal systems, the law is fundamentally anthropocentric. It is structured around human interests and develops an understanding of rights and obligations on the basis of human exercises of agency and autonomy. Some might even argue that the law is ill-equipped to engage with the ecological complexity necessary for meaningful reform, as it tends to reduce dynamic, entangled systems into fixed, manageable categories. As I argue in later chapters, legal narratives often imagine toxicity as if it is "only a violent reflex of pollution, coming on like a wave from elsewhere",[66] leaving scientists to discover the (human) "source" of contamination. As I demonstrate in Chapter 3, when sources of contamination are untraceable or so gradual that it becomes difficult to attribute them to a single cause or activity, the law often characterises its effects as "natural", and therefore beyond the scope of legal intervention.

Accordingly, while green criminology and the ecology of punishment certainly conjure up an image of a volatile and menacing nature, they do so through a lens that assumes that the primary challenge is how humans can

63 Jennie Perey Saxe, 'The Intersection of Incarceration and Injustice: Environmental Burdens in Prison Communities' (2023) 16 Environmental Justice 376.

64 Ben Nevis Barron and others, '"Because We're Dying in Here": A Study of Environmental Vulnerability and Climate Risks in Incarceration Infrastructure' (2024) 7 Environment and Planning E: Nature and Space 2437; Robert Pistone, 'Violations of the Eighth Amendment: How Climate Change Is Creating Cruel and Unusual Punishment' (2022) 28 Hastings Environmental Law Journal 213.

65 Vaughn Ford-Plotkin, 'Climate Change and the Carceral System: How Extreme Weather Threatens Inmates' Eighth Amendment Rights' (2023) 28 Berkeley Journal of Criminal Law 1.

66 Mel Y Chen, *Intoxicated: Race, Disbaility and Chemical Intimacy Across Empire* (Duke University Press 2023) 4.

shield themselves and their most vulnerable populations from its inevitable effects. By centring human agency, Nature is reduced to an inert set of conditions to which humans must adapt, and it is humans that, once again, become the active saboteurs and protectors of Nature. Framed as this mechanical monolith, Nature becomes difficult to imagine as a dynamic convergence of living and non-living communities – plants, microbes, wind, water, animals, metals – each interacting with their environments in ways that reflect their own rhythms, values, and internal logics. Thinking about environmental toxicity and risk takes on new complexities when nature is recognised as lively, fluid, and responsive, what some have called *kinetic*.[67]

Although ecological approaches to punishment expand the focus of carceral harm to include both neighbouring human communities and the surrounding wildlife and biodiversity, they often conceptualise these populations as discrete and unconnected. As a result, punitive effects that are injurious to humans tend to be analysed in isolation from those which are perceived as being harmful to the environment.[68] This anthropocentric partitioning reinforces siloed conceptions of punitive power and impact, rather than recognising punishment as a dispersed, relational force that operates across species boundaries and ecological scales. In many ways, some of which I discuss in the chapters that follow, these approaches to punishment prevent us from seeing how local expressions of punitive power and impact – like the toxic prison – are connected to political economies operating at the national or global scale. Thinking about punishment in such bifurcated terms blocks us from recognising the shared responsibility that we bear for artefacts like the toxic prison, not as an individualised and domestic issue, but as an intergenerational and planetary one.

Punishment as Econormative "Magic"

By now, I hope it is evident that this book shares many of the concerns central to green criminology and the ecology of punishment. What may be less obvious, however, is that one of its central arguments is that environmental exercises of punitive power and impact are normative. When I say that Nature is normative, I mean that it generates its own values and norms, independently of humans, and that these can shape social normativity. In the words of Margaret Davies, from whom this book has drawn tremendous inspiration, "nature contains normative and moral guidance for human action and possibly

67 Thomas Nail, *Theory of the Earth* (Stanford University Press 2021).

68 There are some notable exceptions here including Emma K Russell, 'Prison Expansion in the Plains Grasslands: Coloniality, Ecological Injustice and Carceral Sprawl' (2024) 113 Political Geography 103143; Kelly Struthers Montford, 'Prison Zooing and Conservation: Human and Animal Caging in a Time of Ecological Catastrophe' (2023) 12 Animal Studies Journal.

for human law".[69] Attending to Nature's normativity is thus crucial not only for understanding punishment as a socially embedded practice, but also for interrogating the moral grounds upon which punitive justifications are developed. As Carvalho and Chamberlen have astutely observed, separating "the question of what punishment *is* from what it is *for* is virtually impossible".[70] It is also for this reason that legal theorist Antony Duff and sociological theorist David Garland joined forces to write *The Punishment Reader*, where they, too, remarked:

> All these different ways of writing about punishment are treated as if they are separate disciplines which can proceed independently of one another. The result is that philosophical discussions are often too far removed from the realities of penal practice, while penology and the sociology of punishment are frequently crude or evasive in their handling of complex normative issues.[71]

Moral theories of punishment and real-world penal practice inform, enable, and constrain one another. Consequently, it is not genuinely possible to think about what punishment *ought* to be in the abstract – who it ought to target, how it ought to do so, and where it ought to do so – without thinking concretely about who it *is* targeting, how it *is* doing so, and where it *is* doing so, and then determining whether these exercises of punitive power and impact can be justified. Abstract thinking, particularly when it is grounded in humanist values and anthropocentric assumptions, makes it nearly impossible to grasp, let alone justify, the full extent of human/nonhuman entanglement. Indeed, one might argue that this is precisely why we find ourselves in the current predicament of the Anthropocene.

Within western legal theory, the idea that Nature has normative value may seem controversial, though it is an ancient idea that has informed Indigenous legal theory and practice for many millennia. The normative worlds of many Indigenous communities are constructed through conversation with glaciers and rocks,[72] or by dancing with land and the natural environment.[73]

69 Margaret Davies, *EcoLaw: Legality, Life, and the Normativity of Nature* (Taylor & Francis 2022) 91.

70 Carvalho and Chamberlen (n 7) 13.

71 Antony Duff and David Garland (eds), *A Reader on Punishment* (Oxford University Press 1994) 1.

72 Julie Cruikshank, 'Are Glaciers "Good to Think With"? Recognising Indigenous Environmental Knowledge' (2012) 22 Anthropological Forum 239; Christine M Ami, 'When Waters Rise and Rocks Speak: An Analysis of Indigenous Research Credential Theft by an Ally' (2019) 34 Wicazo Sa Review 54.

73 Juan Alejandro Chindoy Chindoy, 'Dancing as Environmental Aesthetics from Indigenous America' (2021) 12 Roczniki Kulturoznawcze 65; Vincent Clement, 'Dancing Bodies and Indig-

Understandably, the suggestion that western legal systems engage with Nature as a normative force seems as fantastical as invocations of magic or the supernatural. Personally, I think I am all for magic. A magical world where Nature exercises agency and normative force strikes me as no more absurd than the Enlightenment fantasy of a world populated by floating rational minds, all demanding individualised rights while pretending they do not have bodies. Magic, often cast as the impoverished shadow of science in western thought, stands in for phenomena that resist capture by the rationalising imperatives of scientific discourse. Magic is suppressed modes of thought being given the opportunity to enchant. Where science seeks to stabilise, classify, and contain, magic gestures towards resonances, ambiguities, and evocations. Magic affirms the possibility of otherwise worlds.

It is with this invitation for magic that I would like you to approach the rest of this book. Mainstream punishment discourse has a habit of moving between two "orders of reality" that, I believe, allow punitive events and experiences that cannot be categorised as natural or cultural, or easily traced or attributed to certain causes, to disappear from view. In the chapters that follow, I explore how western philosophy and epistemology have contributed to this split view of reality, what kinds of interdependencies that split obscures, and why these hidden connections matter for anyone concerned with punishment theory and practice. What new possibilities does a magical world of bodies, human and nonhuman, living and non-living, jointly constraining and enabling each other's potentialities, make possible for how we conceptualise and practise punishment?

Works Cited

Ami CM, 'When Waters Rise and Rocks Speak: An Analysis of Indigenous Research Credential Theft by an Ally' (2019) 34 Wicazo Sa Review 54.

Armstrong AC, 'Death Row Conditions through an Environmental Justice Lens' (2017) 70 Arkansas Law Review 203.

Barron BN and others, '"Because We're Dying in Here": A Study of Environmental Vulnerability and Climate Risks in Incarceration Infrastructure' (2024) 7 Environment and Planning E: Nature and Space 2437.

Beckett K and Murakawa N, 'Mapping the Shadow Carceral State: Toward an Institutionally Capacious Approach to Punishment' (2012) 16 Theoretical Criminology 221.

Bentham J, *The Panopticon Writings* (Verso Books 2020).

Berg MT and others, 'Losing Years Doing Time: Incarceration Exposure and Accelerated Biological Aging among African American Adults' (2021) 62 Journal of Health and Social Behavior 460.

enous Ontology: What Does the Haka Reveal about the Maori Relationship with the Earth?' (2017) 42 Transactions of the Institute of British Geographers 317.

Bosworth M, *Engendering Resistance: Agency and Power in Women's Prisons* (Routledge 2016).

Bradshaw EA, 'Tombstone Towns and Toxic Prisons: Prison Ecology and the Necessity of an Anti-Prison Environmental Movement' (2018) 26 Critical Criminology 407.

Bruckert C and Munn M, 'Em-Bodying Criminology: (Ex-)Prisoners' Bodies in Time and Space' in Véronique Strimelle and Françoise Vanhamme (eds), *Droits et voix – Rights and Voices* (University of Ottawa Press 2010) 237-254.

Carpenter T, 'The Death Sentence That Is America's Toxic Prison' (2020) 17 Indiana Health Law Review 229.

Carvalho H and Chamberlen A, *Questioning Punishment* (Routledge 2024).

Carvalho H and Chamberlen A, 'Why Punishment Pleases: Punitive Feelings in a World of Hostile Solidarity' (2018) 20 Punishment & Society 217.

Chamberlen A, 'Changing Bodies, Ambivalent Identities, and Women's Punishment' (2017) 12 Feminist Criminology 125.

Chamberlen A, *Embodying Punishment: Emotions, Identities and Lived Experiences in Women's Prisons* (Oxford University Press 2018).

Chen MY, *Intoxicated: Race, Disbaility and Chemical Intimacy Across Empire* (Duke University Press 2023).

Chindoy JAC, 'Dancing as Environmental Aesthetics from Indigenous America' (2021) 12 Roczniki Kulturoznawcze 65.

Clement V, 'Dancing Bodies and Indigenous Ontology: What Does the Haka Reveal about the Maori Relationship with the Earth?' (2017) 42 Transactions of the Institute of British Geographers 317.

Coffman M, 'The Neurological Imprint of Incarceration and Its Effect on Recidivism Notes' (2023) 37 Notre Dame Journal of Law, Ethics & Public Policy 251.

Colucci AR, 'Geographies of Capital Punishment: New Directions and Interventions' (2020) 14 Geography Compass e12548.

Crewe B, 'Depth, Weight, Tightness: Revisiting the Pains of Imprisonment' (2011) 13 Punishment & Society 509.

Crewe B, 'Inside the Belly of the Penal Beast: Understanding the Experience of Imprisonment' (2015) 4 International Journal for Crime, Justice and Social Democracy 50.

Crewe B, 'The Prisoner Society: Power, Adaptation, and Social Life in an English Prison' (2009) 89 Social Forces 3.

Cruikshank J, 'Are Glaciers "Good to Think With"? Recognising Indigenous Environmental Knowledge' (2012) 22 Anthropological Forum 239.

Davies M, *EcoLaw: Legality, Life, and the Normativity of Nature* (Taylor & Francis 2022).

Duff A, *Answering for Crime* (Bloomsbury Publishing 2009).

Duff A, *Trials and Punishments* (CUP Archive 1986).

Duff A and Garland D (eds), *A Reader on Punishment* (Oxford University Press 1994).

Duff RA, *Punishment, Communication and Community* (Oxford University Press 2001).

Durkheim E, *The Division of Labour in Society* (George Simpson tr, Macmillan 1933).

Fassin D and Kutz C (eds), *The Will to Punish* (Oxford University Press 2018).

Feinberg J, 'The Expressive Function of Punishment' in Antony Duff and David Garland (eds), *A Reader on Punishment* (Oxford University Press 1994).

Flew A, 'The Justification of Punishment' (1954) 29 Philosophy 291.

Ford-Plotkin V, 'Climate Change and the Carceral System: How Extreme Weather Threatens Inmates' Eighth Amendment Rights' (2023) 28 Berkeley Journal of Criminal Law 1.

Foucault M, *Discipline and Punish: The Birth of the Prison* (Alan Sheridan tr, Vintage Books 1977).

Gallagher S, 'The Cruel and Unusual Phenomenology of Solitary Confinement' (2014) 5 Frontiers in Psychology.

Gardner J, 'Introduction' in HLA Hart and John Gardner (eds), *Punishment and Responsibility: Essays in the Philosophy of Law* (Oxford University Press 2008).

Garland D, 'Penal Modernism and Postmodernism' in Thomas G Blomberg and Stanley Cohen (eds), *Punishment and Social Control* (Aldine de Gruyter 2003)

Garland D, 'Punishment and Social Solidarity' in Jonathan Simon and Richard Sparks (eds), *The SAGE Handbook of Punishment and Society* (SAGE 2012)

Garland D, 'Sociological Perspectives on Punishment' (1991) 14 Crime and Justice 115.

Garland D, *The Culture of Control: Crime and Social Order in Contemporary Society* (Oxford University Press 2001).

Garland D, 'The Problem of the Body in Modern State Punishment' (2011) 78 Social Research 767.

Gato WE and others, 'Examining the Link Between the Human Microbiome and Antisocial Behavior: Why Criminologists Should Care About Biochemistry, Too' (2018) 39 Deviant Behavior 1191.

Gilani S, 'Sublime Executions and Material Affections: Law, Aesthetics and the Death Penalty' in Imogen Jones and Marc Trabsky (eds), *Routledge Handbook of Law and Death* (Routledge 2024).

Gilani S, 'The Ethics of Capital Punishment and a Law of Affective Enchantment' (2023) 32 Social & Legal Studies 3.

Goffman E, *Asylums: Essays on the Social Situation of Mental Patients and Other Inmates* (Aldine Transaction 2009).

Gopinathan B, Vijayshankar V and Roy S, 'Exploring the Relationship between the Built Environment of Prisons and the Mental Health of Inmates' (2024) 20 International Journal of Prison Health 360.

Greenberg P and Perdue RT, 'Prisons and Pollution: A Nationwide Analysis of Carceral Environmental Inequality' (2025) 72 Social Problems 783.

Hart HL, 'The Presidential Address: Prolegomenon to the Principles of Punishment' (JSTOR 1959).

Hart HLA, 'Introduction' in John Gardner (ed), *Punishment and Responsibility: Essays in the Philosophy of Law* (Oxford University Press 2008).

Helppie-Schmieder B, 'Toxic Confinement: Can the Eighth Amendment Protect Prisoners from Human-Made Environmental Health Hazards Notes and Comments' (2015) 110 Northwestern University Law Review 647.

Herrity K, 'Hearing behind the Door: The Cell as a Portal to Prison Life' in Jennifer Turner and Victoria Knight (eds)*The Prison Cell: Embodied and Everyday Spaces of Incarceration* (2020) 239.

Herrity K, Schmidt BE and Warr J (eds), *Sensory Penalities: Exploring the Senses in Spaces of Punishment and Social Control* (Emerald Publishing 2021).

Herrity KZ, 'Rhythms and Routines: Sounding Order in a Local Men's Prison through Aural Ethnography' (Doctoral, University of Leicester 2019) <https://doi.org/10.25392/leicester.data.10310807.v1> accessed 20 November 2024.

Honderich T, *Punishment: The Supposed Justifications Revisited* (Pluto Press 2006).

Karstedt S, 'Handle with Care: Emotions, Crime and Justice' in Susanne Karstedt, Ian Loader and Heather Strang (eds), *Emotions, Crime and Justice* (Bloomsbury Publishing 2014).

Kleinfeld J, 'Two Cultures of Punishment' (2016) 68 Stanford Law Review 933.

Langmajerová M and others, 'Gut Microbiome in Impulsively Violent Female Convicts' (2024) 84 Neuropsychobiology 1.

'Linking Environmental and Criminal Injustice: The Mining to Prison Pipeline in Central Appalachia | Environmental Justice' <https://www.liebertpub.com/doi/10.1089/env.2017.0027> accessed 11 September 2025.

Logan AC, Mishra P and Prescott SL, 'The Legalome: Microbiology, Omics and Criminal Justice' (2025) 18 Microbial Biotechnology e70129.

Massoglia M, 'Incarceration as Exposure: The Prison, Infectious Disease, and Other Stress-Related Illnesses' (2008) 49 Journal of Health and Social Behavior 56.

McClanahan B and South N, '"All Knowledge Begins with the Senses": Towards a Sensory Criminology' (2020) 60 The British Journal of Criminology 3.

Mead GH, 'The Psychology of Punitive Justice' (1918) 23 American Journal of Sociology 577.

Melossi D and Pavarini M, *The Prison and the Factory (40th Anniversary Edition): Origins of the Penitentiary System* (Springer 2018).

Melton AP, 'Indigenous Justice Systems and Tribal Society Indian Tribal Courts and Justice: A Symposium' (1995) 79 Judicature 126.

Miller C, 'Banishment from within and Without: Analyzing Indigenous Sentencing under International Human Rights Standards' (2004) 80 North Dakota Law Review 253.

Montford KS, 'Prison Zooing and Conservation: Human and Animal Caging in a Time of Ecological Catastrophe' (2023) 12 Animal Studies Journal.

Moore MS, 'The Moral Worth of Retribution' in Ferdinand Schoeman (ed), *Responsibilty, Character, and the Emotions* (Cambridge University Press 2010).

Moran D, *Carceral Geography: The Spaces and Practices of Incarceration* (Ashgate 2015).

Moran D, 'Prisoner Reintegration and the Stigma of Prison Time Inscribed on the Body' (2012) 14 Punishment & Society 564.

Morris N, 'Future of Imprisonment: Toward a Punitive Philosophy, The' (1973) 72 Michigan Law Review 1161.

Nail T, *Theory of the Earth* (Stanford University Press 2021).

Nation Inside: End Mass Incarceration, 'Prison Ecology Project' (2022) <https://nationinside.org/campaign/prison-ecology-project/> accessed 15 June 2024.

Opsal T and others, 'Layered Sites of Environmental Justice: Considering the Case of Prisons* (2023) 93(4) Sociological Inquiry 852.'.

Opsal T, Malin SA and Ellis T, 'Prisons as Law-Violators and Sites of Environmental Injustice' (2023) 31 Critical Criminology 105.

Pistone R, 'Violations of the Eighth Amendment: How Climate Change Is Creating Cruel and Unusual Punishment' (2022) 28 Hastings Environmental Law Journal 213.

'Prisons, Jails, and the Environment: Why Environmentalists Should Care About Mass Incarceration? - Dorceta E. Taylor, 2024' <https://journals.sagepub.com/doi/10.1177/00027642221142206> accessed 11 September 2025.

Raihani NJ, Thornton A and Bshary R, 'Punishment and Cooperation in Nature' (2012) 27 Trends in Ecology & Evolution 288.

Rimke H, 'Constituting Transgressive Interiorities: Nineteenth-Century Psychiatric Readings of Morally Mad Bodies' in Arturo Aldama (ed), *Violence and the Body: Race, Gender, and the State* (Indiana University Press 2003).

Ristroph A, 'Respect and Resistance in Punishment Theory' (2009) 97 California Law Review 601.

Ristroph A, 'State Intentions and the Law of Punishment' (2007) 98 J. Crim. L. & Criminology 1353.

Rothman DJ, *The Discovery of the Asylum: Social Order and Disorder in the New Republic* (2nd edn, Routledge 2017).

Rusche G and Kirchheimer O, *Punishment and Social Structure* (Columbia University Press 2019).

Russell EK, 'Prison Expansion in the Plains Grasslands: Coloniality, Ecological Injustice and Carceral Sprawl' (2024) 113 Political Geography 103143.

Sarat A, *When the State Kills: Capital Punishment and the American Condition* (Princeton University Press 2002).

Saxe JP, 'The Intersection of Incarceration and Injustice: Environmental Burdens in Prison Communities' (2023) 16 Environmental Justice 376.

Shelden RG and Young MV, *Our Punitive Society: Race, Class, Gender, and Punishment in America, Second Edition* (Waveland Press 2020).

Simon J, 'Punishment and the Political Technologies of the Body' in Richard Sparks and Jonathan Simon (eds), *The SAGE Handbook of Punishment and Society* (SAGE 2019).

Simon J and Sparks R, *The SAGE Handbook of Punishment and Society* (SAGE 2012).

Smith C, 'Punishment and Pleasure: Women, Food and the Imprisoned Body' (2002) 50 The Sociological Review 197.

Spohn C, 'Race, Crime, and Punishment in the Twentieth and Twenty-First Centuries' (2015) 44 Crime and Justice 49.

Stuit H, Turner J and Weegels J, *Carceral Worlds: Legacies, Textures and Futures* (Bloomsbury Publishing Plc 2024).

Timmermans S and Gabe J, 'Introduction: Connecting Criminology and Sociology of Health and Illness' (2002) 24 Sociology of Health & Illness 501.

Toman EL, 'Something in the Air: Toxic Pollution in and around U.S. Prisons' (2023) 25 Punishment & Society 867.

Van Den Haag E, 'On Deterrence and the Death Penalty' (1968) 78 Ethics 280.

von Hirsch A, *Doing Justice: The Choice of Punishments* (Hill & Wang 1976).

Wacquant L, 'The Body, the Ghetto and the Penal State' (2009) 32 Qualitative Sociology 101.

Walsh A and Bolen JD, *The Neurobiology of Criminal Behavior: Gene-Brain-Culture Interaction* (Routledge 2016).

White R and Heckenberg D, *Green Criminology: An Introduction to the Study of Environmental Harm* (Routledge 2014).

Whitehead AN, *The Concept of Nature* (Dover Publications 2004).

Wilkes M, 'Toxic Injuries and Toxic Prisons: The Legal Limitations of the Prison Litigation Reform Act Notes' (2024) 25 Rutgers Race & the Law Review [i].

Zedner L, 'Penal Subversions: When Is a Punishment Not Punishment, Who Decides and on What Grounds?' (2016) 20 Theoretical Criminology 3.

2 Posthuman Bodies and Lively Nature

The opening chapter of this book showed that much of the existing punishment scholarship either approaches its study through a disembodied subjectivity that foregrounds abstract moral principles, or from an embodied perspective that remains committed to a transcendental, individual-centred understanding of human life. In doing so, mainstream punishment discourse tends to erase or flatten Nature's role – either ignoring it altogether or reducing it to a passive, mechanical backdrop against which human activity is centralised. It is my view that this framing forecloses recognition of how Nature's forces not only shape the manner in which humans live punishment, as material (bodied) entities, but also neglects the extent to which human and nonhuman normativity are co-emergent.

As I mentioned in the preceding chapter, the idea that nature has normative significance is one that has existed for quite some time. Its philosophical roots can be traced to a much older and established body of Indigenous thought, including the Lakota philosophy of *Mitakuye Oyasin*[1] and the Māori ethics of *kaitiakitanga*.[2] Many Indigenous people across the Americas and Oceania have traditionally understood nature as a living presence – capable of communication, responsiveness, and bearing its own histories and memories.[3] Indigenous philosophies have long foregrounded the relationality of living and non-living phenomena, affirming that humans belong to a "living system" whose forces profoundly shape human life and politics.[4]

But it is only over the last half-century that a growing number of scholars in the western tradition have questioned why human life has been imagined

1 Daniel R Wildcat, 'Foreward' in Soren C. Larsen and Jay T Johnson (eds), *Being Together in Place: Indigenous Coexistence in a More Than Human World* (University of Minnesota Press 2017) ix-xii.

2 Merata Kawharu, 'Kaitiakitanga: A Maori Anthropological Perspective of the Maori Socio-Environmental Ethic of Resource Management' (2000) 109 The Journal of the Polynesian Society 349.

3 Gregory Cajete, 'Philosophy of Native Science' in Anne Waters (ed), *American Indian Thought: Philosophical Essays* (Blackwell Pub 2004).

4 Raymond Pierotti, 'Indigenous Concepts of "Living Systems": Aristotelian "Soul" Meets Constructal Theory' (2015) 6 Ethnobiology Letters 80; Val Plumwood, 'The Concept of Cultural Landscape: Nature, Culture Adn Agency in the Land' (2006) 11 Ethics & the Environment 116.

DOI: 10.4324/9781003367567-3

as a realm of existence separate from that of Nature. In the past two decades especially, these reflections have consolidated into recognisable philosophical perspectives – often gathered under the banners of posthumanism and new materialism – and have developed into shared methodological approaches for rethinking human existence and social life. It is within the philosophical and methodological trajectories of posthumanist and new materialist thinking that my argument about the significance of Nature to punishment theory and practice finds resonance.

While there are many authors who share the general philosophical commitments associated with posthumanist and new materialist thought, not all would describe their worldview using this terminology. For this reason, I want to preface this chapter by noting that posthumanism, in particular, is a deeply contested term,[5] and that both perspectives encompass methodologies that have competing concerns and priorities. Accordingly, both terms are used here for ease of discussion, and not as rigid indicators of conceptual alignment. Nevertheless, at their core, most posthumanists and new materialists are critical of western philosophy's dualist construction of nature, and its prioritisation of human life and interests. They often address this concern in different ways, sometimes exposing the technologically mediated conditions of human life,[6] sometimes by reflecting on the nonhuman capacity for agency and vitality,[7] and sometimes by pointing to the material entanglements between humans and the world(s) they occupy.[8] Whatever path they take, the central warning remains the same: seeing the world in terms of divided and disconnected realms comes at our own peril. Indeed, this alarm has only grown

5 Cary Wolfe, *What Is Posthumanism?*, vol. 8 (University of Minnesota Press 2010) xv; Donna J Haraway, *When Species Meet* (University of Minnesota Press 2008) 17; Manuel De Landa, *Assemblage Theory* (Edinburgh University Press 2016); Alison Ravenscroft, 'Strange Weather: Indigenous Materialisms, New Materialism, and Colonialism' (2018) 5 Cambridge Journal of Postcolonial Literary Inquiry 353.

6 Donna Haraway, *Simians, Cyborgs, and Women: The Reinvention of Nature* (Routledge 1991); Katherine N Hayles, *How We Became Posthuman: Virtual Bodies in Cybernetics, Literature, and Informatics* (University of Chicago Press 2008); Nick Bostrom, *Superintelligence: Path, Dangers, Strategies* (Oxford University Press 2016).

7 Jane Bennett, *Vibrant Matter: A Political Ecology of Things* (Duke University Press 2010); Andreas Philippopoulos-Mihalopoulos, 'Lively Agency: Life and Law in the Anthropocene' in Irus Braverman (ed), *Animals, Biopolitics, Law: Lively Legalities* (Routledge 2015); Sara Ahmed, 'Happy Objects' in Melissa Gregg and Gregory J Seigworth (eds), *The Affect Theory Reader* (Duke University Press 2010); Nancy Tuana, 'Viscous Porosity' in Stacy Alaimo and Susan Hekman (eds), *Material Feminism* (Indiana University Press 2008).

8 Karen Barad, 'Posthumanist Performativity: Toward an Understanding of How Matter Comes to Matter' (2003) 28 Signs: Journal of Women in Culture and Society 801; Samantha Frost, 'Biocultural Creatures' in *Biocultural Creatures* (Duke University Press 2016); Diana Coole and Samantha Frost (eds), *New Materialisms: Ontology, Agency and Politics* (Duke University Press 2010); Donna Haraway, *Staying with the Trouble: Making Kin in the Chthulucene* (Duke University Press 2016).

stronger as we come to terms with the planetary effects of the Anthropocene, and life alongside a natural world that appears capable of generating its own values and norms.

The Nature of Human Existence

Within western Enlightenment philosophy and political theory, humans have long been assigned a special moral status, one that sets them apart from nonhuman beings and often underpins arguments for human exceptionalism. Encapsulated within Descartes' infamous claim "*cogito, ergo sum*" – "I think, therefore I am" – the rational, sentient, conscious subject of Enlightenment thought has become the central figure of a human-centric worldview that positions reason, progress, individual autonomy, and universal truths as the highest ideals of human existence.[9] In Cartesian philosophy, and in its many formulations thereafter, humans are distinguished from the nonhuman world by their capacity for thought and self-awareness.

This mind-centred view of human life found powerful reinforcement in the scientific revolutions of the Enlightenment, where Copernican cosmology and Newtonian physics not only affirmed the human capacity for reason, but positioned humans as uniquely equipped to unravel the mysteries of the physical world. Cast as a curious and methodical observer, the human of Enlightenment thought was capable of both uncovering the natural world's inner logic and harnessing this order for his own ends. As Kirby notes, within this deterministic framework "scientific observation was equated with objectivity [and] perception [was] thought to be a transparent and neutral act".[10] Perception itself became synonymous with truth, and reason was elevated to a moral imperative, an essential tool for human progress, both socially and intellectually.[11] In such a world, where human creativity and rationality reigned supreme, a deterministic nature could never become more than a passive resource to be mastered, ordered, and exploited.

As an objective world of brute facts, nature assumed a valueless and passive configuration, against which the experiential world, conditioned by cultural representation, social values, and historical context, took on new meaning.[12] This distinction between nature and culture also produced a framing of human "being" in dualistic terms. The body was cast as an ahistorical and mechanical instrument that merely registered sensations, while the mind

9 Rene Descartes, *Discourse on Method and Meditations on First Philosophy (4th Edition)* (Donald A Cress tr, Hackett Publishing 1998).

10 Vicki Kirby, *What If Culture Was Nature All Along?* (Edinburgh University Press 2018) 1.

11 Immanuel Kant, *Critique of Pure Reason* (Penguin Books 2007).

12 David Hume, *A Treatise of Human Nature: Being an Attempt to Introduce the Experimental Method of Reasoning into Moral Subjects* (Penguin Books 1985).

was positioned as the reflective and creative interpreter of those sensations. The attribution of meaning thus became political, subject to manipulation and distortion, and producing information that was conceived as more calcula*ting* than calcula*ble*.

For some Enlightenment thinkers, like Hume, this ability to ascribe meaning and value to sensory experience was what added depth and value to human decision-making,[13] and could be considered a defining feature of living beings. Perception was the fundamental feature setting the living and non-living world apart. Accordingly, Enlightenment thought exhibited a general scepticism towards any reduction of biology to physics, or the laws governing "life" to the laws governing "matter" and manifested as a broader rejection of any claim that the physical world possessed a self-organising vitality or *entelechy* akin to that of the evolving organic world.[14]

The Bifurcation of Nature

A central feature of the Enlightenment worldview, as Whitehead describes, is the "bifurcation of nature into two systems of reality": an *a priori* natural world governed by mathematical laws, and an *a posteriori* social world structured through cultural meanings. Since the seventeenth century, this division has fuelled a number of enduring dualisms – nature/culture, human/nonhuman, facts/perception – that continue to structure our systems of knowledge and lead us to perceive the world both as physical matter with measurable attributes on the one hand, and as a realm of socially constructed meanings on the other.[15] We have built our knowledge tools around a world divided across physical and social planes, and our investigation of everything from the microscopic to the cosmic has been organised and framed with these dualisms in mind.

Whitehead's critique of Enlightenment thought in *The Concept of Nature* rests on the view that, in its division of nature from culture, Enlightenment thought diminishes the significance of lived experience, unfairly prioritises the scientific world of "facts", and produces knowledge that is always "unexhaustive" or incomplete.[16] Evidence of this problematic logic can be found within, for instance, the Kantian distinction between *phenomena* (perception) and *noumena* (things-in-themselves), or the view that things possess a material reality that is separate from our perception of it. From Whitehead's view,

13 ibid; David Hume, *An Inquiry Considering Human Understanding* (Oxford University Press 2008).

14 Rudolf Carnap, *An Introduction to the Philosophy of Science* (Martin Gardner ed, Dover Publications 1995) 13–4.

15 Alfred North Whitehead, *The Concept of Nature* (Dover Publications 2004) 21.

16 Ibid., 6–16.

this understanding of reality not only minimises human experience by suggesting that it is necessarily partial (a subjective reality), but because all we have at our disposal *is* perception, it is the only reality that is accessible to us; knowledge about the thing-in-itself remains forever beyond our reach.[17] It is therefore unsurprising that our knowledge systems have prioritised scientific knowledge – knowledge that tries to get to the "essence" of a thing – over experiential knowledge.

Nevertheless, the idea that the world generated through data from microscopes and telescopes remains consistent and stable is a key critique of scientific rationalism. According to Whitehead, dominant scientific projections have flattened the richness of Nature into a mechanical abstraction – where all vitality, intelligence, and responsiveness are reduced to the measurable coordinates of space and time. Nature is no longer seen as a dynamic and adaptive force, but as inert matter, passively obeying external laws.[18] For Whitehead, this is deeply troubling. Such a view of Nature erases the relational intricacies by which the world unfolds, transforming an interconnected and lively cosmos into a sterile collection of isolated substances and events.

The Entanglements between Matter and Meaning

Whitehead's thesis has been taken up by posthuman and new materialist thinkers, who challenge western modernism's mechanistic worldview by tracing the entangled materialities of human and more-than-human experience. Drilling right down to the microcosmic level of the electron, Barad shows how matter, even at the quantum level does not possess fixed and intrinsic properties. Instead, what we call "properties" emerge only through specific material arrangements. In short, the determinate properties of matter are shaped by the instruments used to study it. What Barad's work then suggests is that ways in which we observe and measure the world actively shapes what counts as matter, object, or phenomena. Our observations do not simply reveal pre-existing facts about the things we are observing, they constitute the thing observed. When matter and meaning are understood as inseparable, the physical world emerges as a site of political and ethical significance, with matter itself revealed as plastic and responsive to social and material forces.[19]

Mol makes a similar argument through her study of atherosclerosis (the buildup of plaque in artery walls), explaining how this body-interior process is enacted through a series of materialising practices – patients describing their symptoms, magnetic resonance and microscopic images of arterial

17 Kant (n 11).

18 Whitehead (n 15) 17.

19 Karen Barad, *Meeting the Universe Halfway: Quantum Physics and the Entanglement of Matter and Meaning* (Duke University Press 2007) 148.

cavities, pathology reports on amputated limbs, diagnostic records.[20] It is only through these practices that atherosclerosis takes form and shape, becoming a spatio-temporal entity – fatty deposits within arterial walls. For authors like Mol and Barad, the dynamic plasticity of matter raises the question of whether things exist independently of their practices of mattering. Do we create the things we wish to see by drawing boundaries across entangled processes at the fault lines that "matter" to us? While our apparatuses certainly help us make sense of a chaotic world, we must not lose sight of how our knowledge practices invariably conceal those "resonant somethings" that escape scientific capture.[21] As Barad suggests, the material turn within posthumanist philosophy is not so much about giving matter its due, but about recognising the significance of our processes of "mattering", where we begin to acknowledge the idea of "being" as a kind of "doing". Matter, not as substance, but rather as that which is "produced and productive, generated and generative".[22] Matter as calculat*ing* and not just calcul*able*.

For many authors writing in the posthuman tradition, now loosely organised under the label of science and technology studies, including Stengers, Latour, and Serres, the fashioning of our science according to a particular worldview casts doubt on the idea of scientific objectivity,[23] and conceives of scientific practice as a political exercise. In their reinterpretation of thermodynamics using complex systems theory, Prigogine and Stengers challenge the mechanistic and closed-system perspectives of western science. By focusing on dissipative structures, they argue that nature is self-organising and that order can arise "spontaneously" from disorder. Offering a scientific grounding for thinking about nature as creative, historical, and relational *Order out of Chaos* considers how seemingly minor physical changes can become "amplified into gigantic, structure-breaking waves", rippling outward to transform both natural systems and the social and political networks dependent upon them.[24] This bifurcation of nature has endured precisely because "the scientific mind", Stengers remarks, "requires a very particular

20 Annemarie Mol, *The Body Multiple: Ontology in Medical Practice* (Duke University Press 2002).

21 Andreas Bandak and Daniel M Knight (eds), 'Angel Hair Anthropology with Michel Serres' in *Porous Becomings: Anthropological Engagements with Michel Serres* (Duke University Press 2024) 5.

22 Barad (n 19) 137.

23 Bruno Latour, *Politics of Nature: How to Bring the Sciences into Democracy* (Harvard University Press 2004); Whitehead (n 15); Michel Serres, *Branches: A Philosophy of Time, Event and Advent* (Bloomsbury Academic 2020); Kirby (n 10); Barad (n 19).

24 Ilya Prigogine and Isabelle Stengers, *Order out of Chaos: Man's New Dialogue with Nature* (Verso Books 2017) xvii.

milieu, one that respects its needs, that leaves it free to establish the strictest differentiation between what concerns it – and will be called 'scientific'".[25] To ask scientists to think about anything beyond these very narrow scientific concerns – culture or politics or the arts – "would be to kill what makes them true scientists".[26]

The Co-Constitution of Human and Non human Worlds

A key attribute of both posthumanist and new materialist thought is to bring attention back to the materiality of human existence, the idea of humans as embodied creatures, embedded in, and thus dependent upon, nature. Bringing this together with the material-discursive view of nature proposed by Barad and Mol, thinkers like Latour argue that the human and nonhuman world are co-constitutive; they co-emerge through concrete assemblages. The body thus becomes a site through which the external world impresses itself upon us, *affects* us and, in the process, fundamentally conditions how we become.[27] For Latour, viewing the body as a fixed substance of the self, rather than as an interface where self and world entangle, can act as a conceptual straitjacket, limiting our capacity to attune to the shifting agencies, affects, and relations that shape our world.[28]

This idea that all matter, including humans, exists in the form of assemblages,[29] or as "associations" between "beings" in nature,[30] in technology,[31] and across species,[32] is a common facet of both posthumanist and new materialist thought. Neimanis' *Bodies of Water* illustrates this poignantly through its analysis of the seamless flow between water and bodies. She notes that humans do not merely contain water; we *are* water. Our survival relies on its continual circulation in the form of sweat,

25 Isabelle Stengers, *The Virgin Mary and the Neutrino: Reality in Trouble* (Andrew Goffey tr, Duke University Press 2023) 10.

26 Ibid.

27 Bruno Latour, 'How to Talk About the Body? The Normative Dimension of Science Studies' (2004) 10 Body & Society 205, 205–6.

28 Ibid., 206.

29 De Landa (n 5).

30 Thomas Nail, *Theory of the Earth* (Stanford University Press 2021); Haraway, *Staying with the Trouble: Making Kin in the Chthulucene* (n 8); Frost (n 8); Astrida Neimanis, *Bodies of Water: Posthumanist Feminist Phenomenology* (Bloomsbury 2017).

31 Donna Haraway, 'A Cyborg Manifesto: Science, Technology, and Socialist-Feminism in the Late 20th Century' in *The International Handbook of Virtual Learning Environments* (Springer 2006); Hayles (n 6).

32 Haraway, *When Species Meet* (n 5); Eben Kirksey, *The Multispecies Salon* (Duke University Press 2014).

urine, blood, tears, linking us to wider watery environments, timescales, and beings. As we constantly exchange our watery matter with other humans and nonhumans – "a sea, a cistern, an underground reservoir of once-was-rain"[33] – we become entangled in their "watery politics".[34] These exchanges carry social, legal, economic, and political consequences, and determine who bears the costs of managing these hydrological processes.[35] Humans participate in a planetary hydrological cycle shaped by social and political action, but also exerting its own pressures, norms, and values on human bodies and lives.

Critical to this world-sensitive body is an apprehension of the human's connectedness to both the material movement of the world, but also the political and cultural flows that shape these movements. As Latour observes, something as small as the AIDS virus links sex, psychology, global geography, biotechnology, with local communities, yet the "experts" who write about it "will slice the delicate network traced by the virus for you into tidy compartments where you will find only science, only economy, only social phenomenon, only local news, only sentiment, only sex".[36] This fragmentation obscures two facts: one, that our bodies are open to planetary, rhizomatic[37] movements of matter that unsettle conventional ideas of history and geography, and two that we are active participants in these flows. We are not only affected by the virus, but also its carriers, responders, registers, both socially and materially given that our cellular and immunological processes change in response to it.

Frost's work further shows that bodies are not fixed substances but ongoing electrochemical processes – atoms becoming molecules, molecules becoming proteins, proteins becoming membranes.[38] Different entities – cells, bacteria, enzymes, nerves – make sense of these transformations, and with instruments like microscopes and electrometers we perceive some of this otherwise invisible activity. The body does not need our awareness to function; most of its continual collaborations, resistances, and adaptations occur below consciousness, surfacing only when something goes wrong.[39] In this sense, bodies are "attentive" to their environment, and their responses constitute a

33 Neimanis (n 31) 2.

34 Michael G Kenny, 'A Question of Blood, Race, and Politics' (2006) 61 Journal of the History of Medicine and Allied Sciences 456.

35 Jordan Peccia and Paul Westerhoff, 'We Should Expect More out of Our Sewage Sludge' (2015) 49 Environmental Science & Technology 8271.

36 Bruno Latour, 'Crisis' in Stephanie LeMenager and Teresa Shewry (eds), *Literature and the Environment* (Bloomsbury Publishing 2021) 112.

37 Gilles Deleuze and Felix Guattari, *A Thousand Plateaus* (Brian Massumi tr, University of Minnesota Press 1987).

38 Frost (n 8).

39 Drew Leder, *The Absent Body* (The University of Chicago Press 1990).

kind of meaning-making.[40] What distinguishes a living body, Frost argues, is not its material composition – which is in constant exchange with the world – but the activities and processes it performs.[41] Bodies are dynamic collectives of competing actors, each striving to persist, adapt, and multiply.

Viewing the body as multiplicity, made up of microbes, immune cells, nerves, and membranes with competing interests, reveals how small environmental shifts, like changes in temperature or pressure, can profoundly affect its potential. These interactions between body and world create bodies anew, departures from the natural order, rooted not in randomness but in *latent* or *virtual* possibility.[42] Murphy's concept of latency captures this "not yet", the delay between stimulus and response, or past and present,[43] highlighting how bodies are never static but always in a state of becoming.

As Frost explains, viewing the body as environmentally contingent does not reduce humans to their surroundings. The body is neither a blank slate nor a "fantastical shapeshifter"; its form arises from layered histories of interaction.[44] While porous to planetary flows, bodies also resist, shaped by past biological and political engagements.[45] These histories limit present responses and influence future forms, making the body an iterative trace of intergenerational transformations.[46] As such, bodies reflect not only *what* we are but *who* we are, defining humans as "nomadic subjects" shaped by their material conditions.[47]

Trans-Corporeality

The body, as a product of past interactions and latent potentials, challenges traditional notions of fixed space and time. Alaimo calls all embodied beings "trans-corporeal subjects", whose identities are entangled with "biological, economic, social and political systems…processes and events" across diverse temporal and spatial scales.[48] In the post-COVID world, our bodies

40 Samantha Frost, 'The Attentive Body: How the Indexicality of Epigenetic Processes Enriches Our Understanding of Embodied Subjectivity' (2020) 26 Body & Society 3.

41 Frost (n 8) 75.

42 Gilles Deleuze, *Difference and Repetition* (Paul Patton tr, Bloomsbury 1994).

43 Michelle Murphy, 'Distributed Reproduction, Chemical Violence, and Latency' (*The Scholar & Feminist Online*, 24 September 2013) <https://sfonline.barnard.edu/distributed-reproduction-chemical-violence-and-latency/> accessed 6 July 2024.

44 Frost (n 8) 120.

45 Mark Neocleous, *The Politics of Immunity: Security and the Policing of Bodies* (Verso Books 2022).

46 Frost (n 8) 123.

47 Rosi Braidotti, *Nomadic Subjects: Embodiment and Sexual Difference in Contemporary Feminist Theory* (Columbia University Press 2011).

48 Stacy Alaimo, 'Transcorporeality' in Rosi Braidotti and Maria Hlavajova (eds), *Posthuman Glossary* (Bloomsbury 2018) 435–6.

and sociopolitical relations have been reshaped by global and local forces, including viral spread, vaccine inequities, socioeconomic conditions, and long-COVID's political economy. These changes may even leave inheritable marks on future bodies.[49] For Alaimo, bodies always carry traces of history, social position, place, and even risks.[50]

Accordingly, constructivist conceptions of the body redeploy Enlightenment modernism's nature/culture divide by treating Nature as an "accessory to essentialism" and diminishing "the significance of materiality".[51] As a result, while they "do not deny the material existence of the body…they do tend to focus exclusively on how various bodies have been discursively produced, which casts the body as passive, plastic matter".[52] Instead, trans-corporeality highlights the inseparability of human flesh and environment, offering a space where corporeal and environmental theories productively intersect.[53]

Operating outside the spatial and temporal constraints of scientific inquiry, thinking with the body makes possible new imaginaries. As Neimanis states:

> [a]n adequate understanding of embodiment, then, is not given by simply asking what "a body" is. Instead, we need to be more curious about our politics of location: where is my body? When is it? Why is it? – that is, thanks to what, and whom?…an understanding of one's body – even a rigorously situated one – is multiscalar and multigenerational; porous and palimpsestic.[54]

Thus, posthuman "being" disrupts the body-bound concepts of time, space, and scale, where the "familiar deictics of 'here' and 'there', 'mine' and 'ours', even 'local' and 'global', and 'now' and 'then', which might have once seemed relatively securable, are now queerly torqued".[55] My post-COVID body bears the immunological, biochemical, and neurological imprint of times past, shaped by the activities of a viral entity that moved across corporeal and political boundaries with such ease that what was once far quickly became the intimately near, and the "back then" continues to exist in the "now".

49 Maria Encinosa, 'Embodied Injustices: COVID-19, Race, and Epigenetics' (2021) 2 PANDION: The Osprey Journal of Research and Ideas <https://digitalcommons.unf.edu/pandion_unf/vol2/iss1/3> accessed 29 August 2025.

50 Stacy Alaimo, *Bodily Natures: Science, Environment, and the Material Self* (Indiana University Press 2010) 261.

51 Stacy Alaimo, 'Trans-Corporeal Feminisms and the Ethical Space of Nature' in Stacy Alaimo and Susan Hekman (eds), *Material Feminisms* (Indiana University Press 2008) 237.

52 Ibid., 238.

53 Ibid.

54 Neimanis (n 31) 29.

55 Ibid., 37.

Alaimo argues that trans-corporeality foregrounds environmental justice by revealing how racism, misogyny, and classism are materially inscribed in bodies.[56] Discrimination shapes not only lived experience but also genetic markers, risk factors, and health inequities, what Krieger calls "embodied inequality".[57] The burdens of ill health reflect societal arrangements of power, property, and the interconnection of social and biological life across humans, other species, and the environment.[58] Class, gender, race, and ability influence how bodies materialise, with science, medicine, law, and the military entwined in these oppressive forces.[59] Contrary to the constructivist view, bodies are not passive sites of identity; they are dynamic, "changing and changeable".[60] The trans-corporeal subject frames the body archaeologically, as "a site traversed by strange agencies and immersed within entangled ethical and political relations".[61]

The Vitality of Nature

Alongside these inquiries into the nature of human existence, new materialists have also begun to challenge western conceptions of Nature as passive matter. In their introduction to *New Materialism*, Coole and Frost emphasise both the pervasiveness of material relations and the liveliness or vibrancy of matter. Composed of myriad bodies – animal, chemical, vegetal, microbial, hydrological – all in constant and dynamic intra-action with one another, driven by their own interests in self-persistence, and within ecosystems that are themselves conditioned by electromagnetic, gravitational, atmospheric, and thermodynamic forces and pressures, it becomes difficult to think of Nature as anything *but* active, vibrant, and agentic.[62] Confronted with the inescapable enormity of a world that is constantly moving, transforming, resisting, Coole

56 Alaimo, 'Transcorporeality' (n 49) 436.

57 Nancy Krieger, 'Methods for the Scientific Study of Discrimination and Health: An Ecosocial Approach' (2012) 102 American Journal of Public Health 936, 936.

58 Ibid., 937.

59 Alaimo, 'Transcorporeality' (n 49) 436.

60 Alaimo, 'Trans-Corporeal Feminisms and the Ethical Space of Nature' (n 52) 238.

61 Alaimo, 'Transcorporeality' (n 49) 437.

62 Stuart A West and others, 'The Social Lives of Microbes' (2007) 38 Annu. Rev. Ecol. Evol. Syst. 53; Bennett, *Vibrant Matter: A Political Ecology of Things* (n 7); Jacqueline Dalziell, 'Microbiology as Sociology: The Strange Sociality of Slime' in Vicki Kirby (ed), *What If Culture Was Nature All Along?* (Edinburgh University Press 2018); Merlin Sheldrake, *Entangled Life: How Fungi Make Our Worlds, Change Our Minds, and Shape Our Futures* (Vintage 2021); Isabelle Stengers, 'Receiving the Gift: Earthly Events, Chemical Invariants, and Elemental Powers' in Dimitris Papadopoulos, Maria Puig de la Bellacasa and Natasha Myers (eds), *Reactivating Elements: Chemistry, Ecology, Practice* (Duke University Press 2021); Christopher Donohue and Charles T Wolfe (eds), *Vitalism and Its Legacy in Twentieth Century Life Sciences and Philosophy* (Springer 2023).

and Frost cannot help but ask "how we could be anything *other than* materialist? How could we ignore the power of matter and the way it materialises in our ordinary experiences or fail to acknowledge the primacy of matter in our theories?"[63]

For some authors, the agency or vitality of matter is part of the world's allure, lying in those mysteries that have yet to be uncovered, and allowing Nature to behave in unexpected and unanticipated ways.[64] In her analysis of trash that she finds on the side of the road, Bennett explains the vitality or "dignity" of matter as a thing of value in its own right, "as an existant in excess of its reference to human flaws or projects".[65] To think about these objects as merely "trash, garbage, litter, dirt, debris, filth" reduces them to "the contexts in which (human) subjects set them" and fails to acknowledge their interrelationship with other matter and energies, sunlight, concrete, and human vision and scent.[66] She observes, in failing to acknowledge a thing's individuality, it is impossible to see how each individual thing connects with another to produce something anew, a *scene* made possible only by their assemblage and, most crucially, a scene that *affects*. Scents, tastes, textures, sights, and sounds are *artefacts* of material encounters between the human nose, tongue, ears, eyes, and skin and the particles, pressures, electrical signals, and sound waves emitted by the things around us. How these artefacts stir our bodies into action and feeling is a product of what many authors refer to as "affect", bringing us back into the realm of how matter and meaning become entangled within the lived body.[67]

Affects refers to the intensities felt by the body between sensation and perception. Affect mobilises bodies into action.[68] It has been described as pre-individual bodily forces that heighten or diminish our capacity to act,[69] and as the "non-verbal [and] non-conscious dimensions of experience" engaging sensation, memory, perception, and attention.[70] Affect may prompt sudden reactions – smiling, turning away, or seeking connection – before these responses are consciously recognised. For Massumi, affect is distinct from emotions and refers to a pre-cognitive, visceral experience, expressed through autonomic

63 Coole and Frost (n 8) 1.

64 Jane Bennett, 'The Force of Things: Steps toward an Ecology of Matter' (2004) 32 Political Theory 347; Jane Bennett, *The Enchantment of Modern Life: Attachments, Crossings, and Ethics* (Princeton University Press 2001).

65 Bennett, 'The Force of Things: Steps toward an Ecology of Matter' (n 65) 350.

66 Ibid., 351.

67 Brian Massumi, *Parables for the Virtual: Movement, Affect, Sensation* (Duke University Press 2002); Melissa Gregg, Gregory J Seigworth and Sara Ahmed, *The Affect Theory Reader* (Duke University Press 2010); Kathleen Stewart, *Ordinary Affects* (Duke University Press 2007).

68 Gregg, Seigworth and Ahmed (n 68).

69 Bennett, 'The Force of Things: Steps toward an Ecology of Matter' (n 17) 380.

70 Lisa Blackman and Couze Venn, 'Affect' (2010) 16 Body & Society 7, 8.

bodily reactions at the body's surface and in its interactions with the world,[71] Affect underscores the body's indeterminacy and potential, always pointing to the "virtual", the dormant possibilities of response. As Clough notes, "[i]t is its participation in the virtual that gives affect its autonomy – its escape from the particular thing that embodies it".[72]

For vital materialists, affect describes how things relate to humans and exert power by shaping thoughts and feelings.[73] Sarah Ahmed shows how certain affects, like happiness, "stick" to objects, such as wine or rainbows, through social and cultural histories, guiding us towards normative behaviours.[74] This stickiness reflects a material force binding humans and objects in mutual constitution. Happiness, then, is not just a feeling but a social relation enacted through self-object connections. Bennetts uses the term "thing-power"to describe the force that objects exert on humans and which can prompt action.[75] Things are never inert; they act through their capacities to affect.[76]

The material world can both affect and be affected. Organic matter, in particular, registers environmental conditions, adjusts behaviour, and maintains itself in order to persist. For instance, in Chapter 3, I examine how the fungus *Coccidioides*, survives hostile environments by fragmenting into clusters of individual agents. This adaptive disassembly illustrates Bergson's notion that organic bodies consist of elements that "each live for themselves", with cells sustaining their own distinct properties and functions and forming itself in accordance with its own circumstances.[77] This spontaneity and unpredicability has been described by Bennett as matter's capacity to t "swerve",[78] by Latour as an actant's "causal potential",[79] and by Frost as the body's "attentiveness"to the shifting contours of its environment.[80]

The responsive, creative, and affective power of matter means that things in nature also have the potential to shape human politics. Bennett demonstrates this by discussing the latent power of foods and their ability to condition the decisions that we make about the things we consume, decisions that are largely "unconscious" – stuffing a chip into our mouth without thinking – but which nonetheless have economic and political consequences in terms of

71 Brian Massumi, 'The Autonomy of Affect' (1995) 31 Cultural Critique 83, 85.

72 Clough (n 70) 4.

73 Stewart (n 68) 3.

74 Ahmed (n 7).

75 Bennett, 'The Force of Things: Steps toward an Ecology of Matter' (n 65) 351.

76 Stephen Shaviro, *The Universe of Things* (University of Minnesota Press 2014) 8.

77 Henri Bergson, *Creative Evolution* (Electric Book Company 2000) 40.

78 Bennett, *Vibrant Matter: A Political Ecology of Things* (n 7) 18.

79 Bruno Latour, *Reassembling the Social: An Introduction to Actor-Network Theory* (Oxford University Press 2005).

80 Frost (n 41).

driving the diet industry and shaping global policies on health and obesity.[81] Similarly, scholars of chemical toxicity and environmental pollution argue that toxins carry immense affective force and political power, even though they often remain imperceptible to our senses. Toxic exposure is how humans materially encounter the ongoing legacies of industrial capitalism, neocolonial extraction, climate change, and agricultural industrialisation.[82]

In *Political Matter*, Braun and Whatmore challenge western political theory as:

> [beginning] with (and as) an active purification of human society from the material world, in which the idea of humankind's removal from a state of nature marks the threshold of civilisation and the possibility of political order…the idea that "things" might condition political life is seen to return us to a primitive state, attributing magical qualities to inanimate objects.[83]

Using a defective oil pipeline as an "index of a much wider set of defects of corporate capitalism and its regulation",[84] and the affective registers and "ethical transactions" that plastic bags make possible,[85] contributors to *Political Matter* draw attention to all the ways in which matter and material forces are involved in the "spatiotemporal arrangement of human life",[86] and function as "active parties in the making of social and political associations".[87] For some authors, the sensible artefacts of an encounter – Labelle speaks about sound,[88] but equally others have spoken about odours[89] – can serve as novel approaches to justice because they recognise the performative agency of the things that make themselves available to human bodies through our senses.

81 Bennett, *Vibrant Matter: A Political Ecology of Things* (n 7) 39–51.

82 Stacy Alaimo, *Exposed* (University of Minnesota Press 2016); Michelle Murphy, 'Alterlife and Decolonial Relations' (2017) 32 Cultural Anthropology 494; Mel Y Chen, *Intoxicated: Race, Disability and Chemical Intimacy Across Empire* (Duke University Press 2023).

83 Bruce Braun and Sarah J Whatmore (eds), *Political Matter: Technoscience, Democracy, and Public Life* (University of Minnesota Press 2010) xiv.

84 Andrew Barry, 'Materialist Politics: Metallurgy' in Bruce Braun and Sarah J Whatmore (eds), *Political Matter: Technoscience, Democracy, and Public Life* (University of Minnesota Press 2010) 90–1.

85 Gay Hawkins, 'Plastic Materialities' in Bruce Braun and Sarah J Whatmore (eds), *Political Matter: Technoscience, Democracy, and Public Life* (University of Minnesota Press 2010) 120.

86 Braun and Whatmore (n 86) xii.

87 Ibid., xiii–xiv.

88 Brandon LaBelle, *Acoustic Justice: Listening, Performativity, and the Work of Reorientation* (Bloomsbury 2021).

89 Dayna Nadine Scott, '"We Are the Monitors Now": Experiential Knowledge, Transcorporeality and Environmental Justice' (2016) 25 Social & Legal Studies 261; Dayna Scott, 'The Smell of Neglect: A Transcorporeal Feminism for Environmental Justice' in *Sensing Law* (Routledge 2016).

In speaking about the nonhuman world as active, agentic, and political, posthumanism and new materialism always run the risk of instrumentalising humans. However, as Bennett notes, the risk of this:

> might…be mitigated when [it] is combined with the attempt to enhance the ethical standing of things. The danger of reducing subjects to "mere objects" is most acute…in a materialism in which things are always already on their way to becoming trash (where materiality is conceived as the dead other to life).[90]

In short, when the dividing lines between subjects and objects remain stark. Thus, in connecting human and nonhuman existence I am not arguing that things have a moral and ethical status equivalent to humans, but that they are not merely "objects", or instruments for human political ends. Things have value, they have a vibrancy that cannot be reduced to the ends they serve in the pursuit of human desires and needs. But more importantly, they have the power to shape human social and ethical life. As a result, we must take seriously the opportunity to, as Haraway invites, "make kin" with Nature, form multispecies ethical alliances in mutual pursuit of ecological justice.

Ecolegal Justice

In his beautifully poignant book about how the Earth comes into being, Thomas Nail proposes a kinetic understanding of the cosmos and explains how much of what we recognise as the substance of the earth – its plants, rocks, even its climate – materialise through tensional patterns of motion and interaction. Substance emerges through processes of differentiation between different forces. Vegetality, minerality, and atmospherics are just some of the geokinetic processes that continuously configure, deconfigure, and reconfigure the Earth that we have been taught to think about as "homeostatic" or "capable of being stabilised by life".[91] According to Nail, the Earth has never been an "ahistorical substance…a passive object or product of natural, divine, or mechanical laws".[92] Volcanoes, glaciers, hurricanes, droughts, and floods are just some of the geological and atmospheric phenomena that have shaped Earth physically *and* culturally.[93] These phenomena, he writes, "should draw

90 Bennett, 'The Force of Things: Steps toward an Ecology of Matter' (n 65) 360.

91 Nail (n 31) 7.

92 Ibid., 5.

93 Mark Carey, *In the Shadow of Melting Glaciers* (Oxford University Press 2010); David K Chester, 'Volcanoes, Society, and Culture' in Gerald GJ Ernst and Joan Marti (eds), *Volcanoes and the Environment* (Cambridge University Press 2005); Clive Oppenheimer, *Mountains of Fire* (Hachette 2023).

our attention to a hidden dimension of Earth's fundamental instability"[94] and the implications this instability, indeterminacy, has for human life.

But it is not only that Nature exerts pressures on human life. Indeed, theories of how we are living at a moment in time that can be described as the Anthropocene have made it increasingly clear that human activity is also very much part of the tensional politics of Earth's becoming. What human societies believe, the decisions that they make, and the actions that they carry out reverberate through and across Earth. As Nail writes, "multiple human structures shape contemporary reality. These structures are, in turn, conditioned by other real, terrestrial processes that have been around since long before humans walked the earth".[95] By human "structures", Nail not only refers to social institutions and physical activity but also intellectual processes and political-economic formations. Nail, in the spirit of arguments that have already been advanced by Whitehead, Stengers, and Latour, explains how the Earth sciences, the body of work that purports to describe how the Earth operates, the mechanical laws by which it is governed, has a hand in jointly creating Earth as a substance, as a *thing* that matters, an object that has consequences and effects.[96] Similarly, many posthumanists have considered the ways in which capitalism, colonialism, resource extractivism, agricultural industrialisation, corporatism, and globalisation have conditioned Earth's movements.[97]

If we recognise that the material world possesses agency, affective force, and political import – that it acts with us and through us – then its movements and transformations cannot be treated as merely external to how we conduct ourselves and live our lives. Rather, they must be understood as essential to the conditions through which (human) norms are generated and sustained. How Nature behaves has relevance for human law and human normativity. Nature's movements constrain and enable the social activity of humans, and for this reason, we can say that those movements have normative force.

In *Ecolaw*, Margaret Davies describes norm-creation as purposeful, iterative, and relational, emerging from repeated behaviours and assemblages. Thinking of norms this way highlights that Nature itself is normative. The natural processes of decay, water cycles, and plant lifecycles establish conditions for life by shaping what is possible. Nature's normativity arises from its inherent patterns of ordering, directing, enabling, and constraining, as seen in

94 Nail (n 31) 7.
95 Ibid., 9.
96 Ibid., 22–3.
97 Dipesh Chakrabarty, 'The Human Condition in the Anthropocene' in *Tanner Lectures in Human Values* (Yale University 2015) https://tannerlectures.org/lectures/the-human-condition-in-the-anthropocene/ accessed 16 August 2025; Antoine Acker, Olaf Kaltmeier and Anne Tittor, 'Negotiating Nature: Imaginaries, Interventions, and Resistance' (2016) 9(2) Research Volume 5–24. Austin Zeiderman, *Artery: Racial Ecologies on Colombia's Magdalena River* (Duke University Press 2025).

rivers that *must* flow, bodies that *must* metabolise, and energy that *must* dissipate. Purpose here requires no intention; it is expressed through self-organisation, with Nature behaving in ways that favour growth, replication, survival, and non-random continuity.[98]

For Davies, norms are not fixed prescriptions but relational effects of interactions among humans, nonhumans, technology, and the environment. For this reason, patterns of behaviour that normalise a way of existing do not require intention, deliberation, or self-awareness.[99] As she notes, "normative creation and co-creation are more difficult to perceive in relation to nonlife because the creative agential aspect appears to be entirely on the side of the human".[100] Nevertheless, the fact that nature's normative patterns of behaviour are capable of shifting, responding, and adapting to environmental situations is indicative of the creative agency of nature.[101] Nature does not operate according to indifferent and mechanical laws; it is vibrant. Humans inhabit a complex and dynamic *nomos*.

Recognising the normativity of nature has profound implications for human law, not least because it can significantly influence how and with whom we deliberate in creating our own system of norms. For Davies, law is not a fixed set of rules but a responsive practice embedded in dynamic material flows. While this is clear with living entities, as I explore in Chapter 3 with my discussion of fungi, it becomes more complex and controversial when applied to non-living matter, as Chapter 4's discussion of chemicals and the death penalty illustrates. Davies encourages an imagining of normativity that is plural, overlapping, and distributed across legal, social, material, and ecological sites. Norms are processes of configuring, deconfiguring, and reconfiguring within an interdependent world, where human life is entangled with nonhuman life and ecological processes. Chapters 3 and 4 show that assuming humans are the sole norm-generating species often blinds us to Nature's dynamicity; this oversight underpins the ecological and cultural traumas of the Anthropocene.[102]

Nature's purposeful patterns show that it is neither neutral, static, nor indifferent, as western philosophy often assumes. Recognising nature's inherent dynamism challenges the idea that human norms can be absolute or universal,

98 Margaret Davies, *EcoLaw: Legality, Life, and the Normativity of Nature* (Taylor & Francis 2022) 62–70.

99 Ibid., 73.

100 Ibid., 77.

101 Ibid., 58–9.

102 Haraway, *Staying with the Trouble: Making Kin in the Chthulucene* (n 8); Thomas Hylland Eriksen, 'The Loss of Diversity in the Anthropocene Biological and Cultural Dimensions' (2021) 3 Frontiers in Political Science; Rob Nixon, 'The Promise and Pitfalls of the Epochal Era' in Gregg Mitman, Marco Armiero and Robert S Emmett (eds), *Future Remains: A Cabinet of Curiosities for the Anthropocene* (University of Chicago Press 2022); Clive Hamilton, 'Define the Anthropocene in Terms of the Whole Earth' (2016) 536 Nature 251.

highlighting the need for legal frameworks that respond to ecological realities. Davies' concept of "ecolaw" frames human norms as relational and conditioned by natural teleologies, operating within ecological constraints. Law, in this view, is situated, responsive, and attuned to changing environmental conditions.

The following chapters explore how being entangled in Earth's dynamic processes shapes punitive practice and experience. Two case studies are used to illustrate this. The first examines ecological forces in the experience of prisoner disease in California's Central Valley and the second considers the chemical ecologies of the death penalty. In both cases, norms of punishment reflect a dominant western view of Nature as static and neutral, resulting in practices that alienate us from our institutions and obscure global power dynamics. These norms leave us disempowered, swinging between feelings of helplessness in the face of an unpredictable nature, and overconfidence before a rigid and mechanical one. Ultimately, responding effectively requires attending to nature itself and rethinking human normativity in dialogue with its inherent patterns.

Works Cited

Acker A, Kaltmeier, Olaf and Tittor A, 'Negotiating Nature: Imaginaries, Interventions, and Resistance' (2016) 9(2) Research.

Ahmed S, 'Happy Objects' in Melissa Gregg and Gregory J Seigworth (eds), *The Affect Theory Reader* (Duke University Press 2010).

Alaimo S, *Bodily Natures: Science, Environment, and the Material Self* (Indiana University Press 2010).

Alaimo S, *Exposed* (University of Minnesota Press 2016).

Alaimo S, 'Trans-Corporeal Feminisms and the Ethical Space of Nature' in Stacy Alaimo and Susan Hekman (eds), *Material Feminisms* (Indiana University Press 2008).

Alaimo S, 'Transcorporeality' in Rosi Braidotti and Maria Hlavajova (eds), *Posthuman Glossary* (Bloomsbury 2018).

Bandak A and Knight DM (eds), 'Angel Hair Anthropology with Michel Serres' in *Porous Becomings: Anthropological Engagements with Michel Serres* (Duke University Press 2024).

Barad K, *Meeting the Universe Halfway: Quantum Physics and the Entanglement of Matter and Meaning* (Duke University Press 2007).

Barad K, 'Posthumanist Performativity: Toward an Understanding of How Matter Comes to Matter' (2003) 28 Signs: Journal of Women in Culture and Society 801.

Barry A, 'Materialist Politics: Metallurgy' in Bruce Braun and Sarah J Whatmore (eds), *Political Matter: Technoscience, Democracy, and Public Life* (University of Minnesota Press 2010).

Bennett J, *The Enchantment of Modern Life: Attachments, Crossings, and Ethics* (Princeton University Press 2001).

Bennett J, 'The Force of Things: Steps toward an Ecology of Matter' (2004) 32 Political Theory 347.

Bennett J, *Vibrant Matter: A Political Ecology of Things* (Duke University Press 2010).

Bergson H, *Creative Evolution* (Electric Book Company 2000).

Blackman L and Venn C, 'Affect' (2010) 16 Body & Society 7.

Bostrom N, *Superintelligence: Path, Dangers, Strategies* (Oxford University Press 2016).

Braidotti R, *Nomadic Subjects: Embodiment and Sexual Difference in Contemporary Feminist Theory* (Columbia University Press 2011).

Braun B and Whatmore SJ (eds), *Political Matter: Technoscience, Democracy, and Public Life* (University of Minnesota Press 2010).

Cajete G, 'Philosophy of Native Science' in Anne Waters (ed), *American Indian thought: philosophical Essays* (Blackwell Pub 2004).

Carey M, *In the Shadow of Melting Glaciers* (Oxford University Press 2010).

Carnap R, *An Introduction to the Philosophy of Science* (Martin Gardner ed, Dover Publications 1995).

Chakrabarty D, 'The Human Condition in the Anthropocene' in *Tanner Lectures in Human Values* (Yale University 2015) <https://tannerlectures.org/wp-content/uploads/sites/105/2024/05/Chakrabarty-manuscript.pdf> accessed 16 August 2025.

Chen MY, *Intoxicated: Race, Disability and Chemical Intimacy Across Empire* (Duke University Press 2023).

Chester DK, 'Volcanoes, Society, and Culture' in Gerald GJ Ernst and Joan Marti (eds), *Volcanoes and the Environment* (Cambridge University Press 2005).

Clough PT, 'The Affective Turn: Political Economy, Biomedia and Bodies' (2008) 25 Theory, Culture & Society 1.

Coole D and Frost S (eds), *New Materialisms: Ontology, Agency and Politics* (Duke University Press 2010).

Dalziell J, 'Microbiology as Sociology: The Strange Sociality of Slime' in Vicki Kirby (ed), *What if Culture was Nature All Along?* (Edinburgh University Press 2018).

Davies M, *EcoLaw: Legality, Life, and the Normativity of Nature* (Taylor & Francis 2022).

De Landa M, *Assemblage Theory* (Edinburgh University Press 2016).

Deleuze G, *Difference and Repetition* (Paul Patton tr, Bloomsbury 1994).

Deleuze G and Guattari F, *A Thousand Plateaus* (Brian Massumi tr, University of Minnesota Press 1987).

Descartes R, *Discourse on Method and Meditations on First Philosophy (4th Edition)* (Donald A Cress tr, Hackett Publishing 1998).

Donohue C and Wolfe CT (eds), *Vitalism and Its Legacy in Twentieth Century Life Sciences and Philosophy* (Springer 2023).

Encinosa M, 'Embodied Injustices: COVID-19, Race, and Epigenetics' (2021) 2 PANDION: The Osprey Journal of Research and Ideas <https://digitalcommons.unf.edu/pandion_unf/vol2/iss1/3> accessed 29 August 2025.

Eriksen TH, 'The Loss of Diversity in the Anthropocene Biological and Cultural Dimensions' (2021) 3 Frontiers in Political Science 1.

Frost S, 'Biocultural Creatures', *Biocultural Creatures* (Duke University Press 2016).

Frost S, 'The Attentive Body: How the Indexicality of Epigenetic Processes Enriches Our Understanding of Embodied Subjectivity' (2020) 26 Body & Society 3.

Gregg M, Seigworth GJ and Ahmed S, *The Affect Theory Reader* (Duke University Press 2010).

Hamilton C, 'Define the Anthropocene in Terms of the Whole Earth' (2016) 536 Nature 251.

Haraway D, 'A Cyborg Manifesto: Science, Technology, and Socialist-Feminism in the Late 20th Century' in *The International Handbook of Virtual Learning Environments* (Springer 2006).

Haraway D, *Simians, Cyborgs, and Women: The Reinvention of Nature* (Routledge 1991).

Haraway D, *Staying with the Trouble: Making Kin in the Chthulucene* (Duke University Press 2016).

Haraway DJ, *When Species Meet* (University of Minnesota Press 2008).

Hawkins G, 'Plastic Materialities' in Bruce Braun and Sarah J Whatmore (eds), *Political Matter: Technoscience, Democracy, and Public Life* (University of Minnesota Press 2010).

Hayles KN, *How We Became Posthuman: Virtual Bodies in Cybernetics, Literature, and Informatics* (University of Chicago Press 2008).

Hume D, *A Treatise of Human Nature: Being an Attempt to Introduce the Experimental Method of Reasoning into Moral Subjects* (Penguin Books 1985).

Hume D, *An Inquiry Considering Human Understanding* (Oxford University Press 2008).

Kant I, *Critique of Pure Reason* (Penguin Books 2007).

Kawharu M, 'Kaitiakitanga: A Maori Anthropological Perspective of the Maori Socio-Environmental Ethic of Resource Management' (2000) 109 The Journal of the Polynesian Society 349.

Kenny MG, 'A Question of Blood, Race, and Politics' (2006) 61 Journal of the History of Medicine and Allied Sciences 456.

Kirby V, *What If Culture Was Nature All Along?* (Edinburgh University Press 2018).

Kirksey E, *The Multispecies Salon* (Duke University Press 2014).

Krieger N, 'Methods for the Scientific Study of Discrimination and Health: An Ecosocial Approach' (2012) 102 American Journal of Public Health 936.

LaBelle B, *Acoustic Justice: Listening, Performativity, and the Work of Reorientation* (Bloomsbury 2021).

Larsen SC, Johnson JT and Wildcat DR, 'Foreward' in *Being Together in Place: Indigenous Coexistence in a More Than Human World* (University of Minnesota Press 2017).

Latour B, 'Crisis' in Stephanie LeMenager and Teresa Shewry (eds), *Literature and the Environment* (Bloomsbury Publishing 2021).

Latour B, 'How to Talk About the Body? The Normative Dimension of Science Studies' (2004) 10 Body & Society 205.

Latour B, *Politics of Nature: How to Bring the Sciences into Democracy* (Harvard University Press 2004).

Latour B, *Reassembling the Social: An Introduction to Actor-Network Theory* (Oxford University Press 2005).

Leder D, *The Absent Body* (University of Chicago Press 1990).

Massumi B, *Parables for the Virtual: Movement, Affect, Sensation* (Duke University Press 2002).

Massumi B, 'The Autonomy of Affect' (1995) 31 Cultural Critique 83.

Mol A, *The Body Multiple: Ontology in Medical Practice* (Duke University Press 2002).

Murphy M, 'Alterlife and Decolonial Relations' (2017) 32 Cultural Anthropology 494.

Murphy M, 'Distributed Reproduction, Chemical Violence, and Latency' (*The Scholar & Feminist Online*, 24 September 2013) <https://sfonline.barnard.edu/distributed-reproduction-chemical-violence-and-latency/> accessed 6 July 2024.

Nail T, *Theory of the Earth* (Stanford University Press 2021).
Neimanis A, *Bodies of Water: Posthumanist Feminist Phenomenology* (Bloomsbury 2017).
Neocleous M, *The Politics of Immunity: Security and the Policing of Bodies* (Verso Books 2022).
Nixon R, 'The Promise and Pitfalls of the Epochal Era' in Gregg Mitman, Marco Armiero and Robert S Emmett (eds), *Future Remains: A Cabinet of Curiosities for the Anthropocene* (University of Chicago Press 2022).
Oppenheimer C, *Mountains of Fire* (Hachette 2023).
Peccia J and Westerhoff P, 'We Should Expect More out of Our Sewage Sludge' (2015) 49 Environmental Science & Technology 8271.
Philippopoulos-Mihalopoulos A, 'Lively Agency: Life and Law in the Anthropocene' in Irus Braverman (ed), *Animals, Biopolitics, Law: Lively Legalities* (Routledge 2015).
Pierotti R, 'Indigenous Concepts of "Living Systems": Aristotelian "Soul" Meets Constructal Theory' (2015) 6 Ethnobiology Letters 80.
Plumwood V, 'The Concept of Cultural Landscape: Nature, Culture Adn Agency in the Land' (2006) 11 Ethics & the Environment 116.
Prigogine I and Stengers I, *Order out of Chaos: Man's New Dialogue with Nature* (Verso Books 2017).
Ravenscroft A, 'Strange Weather: Indigenous Materialisms, New Materialism, and Colonialism' (2018) 5 Cambridge Journal of Postcolonial Literary Inquiry 353.
Scott D, 'The Smell of Neglect: A Transcorporeal Feminism for Environmental Justice' in Sheryl Hamilton, Diana Majury, Dawn Moore, Neil Sargent and Christiane Wilke (eds) *Sensing Law* (Routledge 2017 Chapter 7.
Scott DN, '"We Are the Monitors Now": Experiential Knowledge, Transcorporeality and Environmental Justice' (2016) 25 Social & Legal Studies 261.
Serres M, *Branches: A Philosophy of Time, Event and Advent* (Bloomsbury Academic 2020).
Shaviro S, *The Universe of Things* (University of Minnesota Press 2014).
Sheldrake M, *Entangled Life: How Fungi Make Our Worlds, Change Our Minds, and Shape Our Futures* (Vintage 2021).
Stengers I, 'Receiving the Gift: Earthly Events, Chemical Invariants, and Elemental Powers' in Dimitris Papadopoulos, Maria Puig de la Bellacasa and Natasha Myers (eds), *Reactivating Elements: Chemistry, Ecology, Practice* (Duke University Press 2021).
Stengers I, *The Virgin Mary and the Neutrino: Reality in Trouble* (Andrew Goffey tr, Duke University Press 2023).
Stewart K, *Ordinary Affects* (Duke University Press 2007).
Tuana N, 'Viscous Porosity' in Stacy Alaimo and Susan Hekman (eds), *Material Feminism* (Indiana University Press 2008).
West SA and others, 'The Social Lives of Microbes' (2007) 38 Annu. Rev. Ecol. Evol. Syst. 53.
Whitehead AN, *The Concept of Nature* (Dover Publications 2004).
Wolfe C, *What Is Posthumanism?*, vol. 8 (University of Minnesota Press 2010).
Zeiderman A, *Artery: Racial Ecologies on Colombia's Magdalena River* (Duke University Press 2025).

3 Fungal Normativity and Prisoner Disease

Beneath the dry earth of California's Central Valley lies a hidden world, vast, intricate, and largely unseen. This underground landscape, which may appear barren and lifeless, is teeming with activity capable of shaping the lives of those who live above ground in significant and consequential ways. This chapter explores the subterranean life and politics of coccidioidomycosis, and how it comes to shape human life and politics. Commonly known as Valley Fever, coccidioidomycosis is a disease caused by the inhalation of airborne spores (arthroconidia) of the soil-dwelling fungus *Coccidioides* (Cocci). Released into the air when their soil habitats are disturbed, Cocci spores can be easily inhaled by animals and people. Once inhaled, the spores can settle in the lungs and begin to multiple, triggering the body's immune response and potentially leading to infection. While most infections resolve on their own without any medical intervention, in some cases infections can escalate to more serious forms of disease, causing symptoms as mild as fatigue and fever to as serious as skin lesions, chronic joint pain, and respiratory distress. Though symptoms can be managed using antifungal medication, Cocci spores are never fully eradicated from their host's body and can lie dormant within these quarters for years.[1] In the most acute cases of disseminated disease, when the fungus moves out of the lungs to infect other vital organs, bones, and the central nervous system, Valley Fever disease can be fatal.

Interestingly, although Cocci is often described as endemic to the desert Southwest of the United States, with the San Joaquin Valley being labelled "hyperendemic", infection rates among prisoners in the Valley remain disproportionately elevated compared with the general population.. Despite the disproportionate distribution of disease across incarcerated populations, when prisoners have challenged the constitutionality of the heightened risk they face, state courts have been hesitant to hold correctional institutions legally liable. In the courts' view, exposure to the disease-causing fungus is geographically situated, and thus prisoners face no more risk than other residents of the San Joaquin Valley.

1 Nancy F Crum, 'Coccidioidomycosis: A Contemporary Review' (2022) 11 Infectious Diseases and Therapy 713; Jan V Hirschmann, 'The Early History of Coccidioidomycosis: 1892–1945' (2007) 44 Clinical Infectious Diseases 1202, 1205.

DOI: 10.4324/9781003367567-4

In the sections that follow I examine how the courts' understanding of Valley Fever relies on a vision of Nature that is stable and stationary, rather than creative and attentive. By failing to consider the material history of how the San Joaquin Valley became a "hyperendemic zone", the courts portray the unequal distribution of disease burden among prisoners as the result of either human-driven environmental disruptions - treated as unavoidable or disconnected from penal institutions - or genetic predispositions that make certain groups more susceptible to disease. Either way, the court's handling of this disease leads to interventions that do little to address the structural conditions that enable Valley Fever and worsen its effects for already marginalised populations. .

Using an ecological approach that centres fungal agency and environmental responsiveness, this chapter shows how Valley Fever is not simply a medical condition affecting prisoners, but an expression of multispecies entanglement with trans-corporeal consequences. Valley Fever in the prison is an issue of environmental injustice, rooted in the political economies of industrial agriculture and neoliberal capitalism, and its management requires the law to think more deeply about the mutually constitutive relationship between nature and culture, and how human politics provokes (and is itself configured by) ecological re-patternings.

Exposure to Valley Fever as Cruel and Unusual Punishment

Between 2006 and 2016, the California Department of Corrections and Rehabilitation (CDCR) found itself at the centre of a silent public health disaster. Within two of its most densely populated correctional facilities, Avenal and Pleasant Valley State Prison (PVSP), cases of Valley Fever were rising at an alarming pace.[2] At their peak, these prisons recorded infection rates that were 1,000 times greater than those observed in the general population,[3] and as morbidity rates approached 17 percent and fatalities mounted, it was increasingly clear that the disease had reached epidemic proportions.

The Valley Fever outbreak at Avenal and PVSP disproportionately affected Black, Asian, and Native American prisoners, who experienced more severe

2 John Dannenberg, 'Valley Fever Declared a Public Health Emergency at Two California Prisons; Court Orders Prisoner Transfers' <https://www.prisonlegalnews.org/news/2013/jul/15/valley-fever-declared-a-public-health-emergency-at-two-california-prisons-court-orders-prisoner-transfers/>; Kerry Klein, 'Before COVID-19, A California State Prison Battled Valley Fever' (*Science Friday*) <https://www.sciencefriday.com/articles/avenal-prison-valley-fever/> accessed 20 June 2025.

3 *Jackson v Brown* [2015] Case No 1:13-cv-1055-LJO-SAB (ED Cal) 24; 'Valley Fever: An Incurable Illness in the Dust' (*BBC News,* 16 July 2013) <https://www.bbc.com/news/magazine-23166839> accessed 2 October 2025.

symptoms and higher risk of disseminated disease. For over a decade now, current and former inmates of Avenal and PVSP suffering from the chronic effects of Valley Fever have been collectively suing the CDCR. It is their claim that the state's failure to either exclude high-risk inmates from prisons located in hyperendemic zones or implement remedial measures to lower their risk of infection directly contributed to the raised incidence of prisoner disease and death during this ten-year period. Inmates from high-risk groups allege that the CDCR's negligence led to substantially different conditions of punishment for them, compared to others, and that the state's failure to take preventative measures amounted to discriminatory treatment in direct violation of the plaintiffs' Eighth Amendment rights against cruel and unusual punishment and Fourteenth Amendment rights to equal protection under the law.[4]

In the vast majority of these cases, courts in the United States have ruled against the plaintiffs, citing the doctrine of qualified immunity. Under this rule, state officials are protected from civil liability in the course of performing their duties, unless plaintiffs are able to establish that they have a constitutional right to be protected from exposure, and that prison officials were aware of this right and acted contrary to it with deliberate indifference, malicious intent, or wilful negligence.[5] A successful Eighth Amendment challenge requires plaintiffs to demonstrate that their risk of toxic exposure is one that is not equally borne by the general public,[6] and that the conditions of confinement significantly heightened their risk of exposure compared to surrounding communities.[7]

In these legal accounts of Valley Fever, the high infection rates among inmates are typically explained in three ways. One explanation focuses on routine human activities, such as ongoing construction near the prisons, which may have stirred up and increased the concentration of airborne fungal spores inhaled by prisoners.[8] A second explanation suggests that inmates are more likely to report symptoms than the general public, and prison medical staff are better equipped to diagnose the disease.[9] Finally, in some cases, the higher rates of infection in Avenal and PVSP are attributed to the simple fact that

4 *Beagle v Schwarzenegger* [2014] Case No 1:14-cv-00430- LJO-SAB (ED Cal); *Chaney v Beard* Case No 1:14-cv-00369-MJS (ED Cal); *Bates v Schwarzenegger* [2020] Case No 19-17094 (9th Cir); *Hines v Youseff* [2019] 9th Cir 914 F.3d 1218; *Nawabi v Cates* [2015] Case No 1:13-cv-272-LJO-SAB (ED Cal); *Cunningham v Kramer* [2016] 178 F Supp 3d 999 (ED Cal); *Jackson v. Brown* (n 3); *Franklin v Giurbino* [2018] Case No 15-cv-04755-YGR (PR) (ND Cal); *Smith v Schwarzenegger* [2015] Case No: 1:14-cv-00060-LJO-SAB. It should be noted that several of the pre-2015 cases on the issue of qualified immunity were consolidated under *Smith v. Schwarzenegger.*

5 *Jackson v. Brown* (n 3); *Cunningham v. Kramer* (n 4).

6 *Jackson v. Brown* (n 3) 25.

7 Ibid., 27, 33.

8 *Hines v. Youseff* (n 4) 1226.

9 Ibid.

these particular institutions are in regions where the spores are "naturally more virulent".[10] Ultimately, these explanations are grounded in a dualistic conception of the disease; one either based in a static "natural" realm imagined as external to human influence, or a dynamic "cultural" realm governed by individual and institutional agency.

Within this legal framing, infection became a stochastic event, and the severity of illness and its preponderance amongst particular social groups reduced to a biological quirk of individual bodies rather than a consequence of structural inequality. High-risk prisoners were collapsed into a generalised category of biologically vulnerable bodies, indistinct from others in the surrounding population, all equally at risk of acquiring disseminated disease from a fungus that "naturally exist[ed]"[11] or "naturally occur[red]"[12] in the regions where the two prisons were located. The higher rates of severe illness and death from Valley Fever among prisoners were attributed to inherent genetic susceptibility, with the suggestion that prisons disproportionately housed the kinds of (unhealthy and raced) bodies that were naturally more vulnerable to serious infection. The courts' reading of Valley Fever construed the prevalence of infection as a matter of *where* bodies were (in an endemic zone),[13] and *what* they were (biologically predisposed), while the *who* of race, class, and political status were neglected. That those deemed biologically vulnerable were disproportionately Black, Brown, Indigenous, and poor – a demographic overrepresented in California's prison system[14] – was rendered irrelevant under a judicial logic that insisted on the separability of nature and law, environment and ethics.

The legal accounts of Valley Fever in the prison imagine nature as an object of study and control, a passive and mechanical system that propels itself without any care or concern for the human world it touches. By describing Cocci – the fungus responsible for causing disease – as "naturally occurring"[15]and endemic or "native" to Central California, and framing Valley Fever as a "common fact of contemporary life",[16] the courts render this fungus inert, stripping it of any vitality or capacity for agency. We are given the impression that this organism's lifecycle has nothing of interest to contribute to legal discussions about ethical punishment. But Cocci are creative creatures. Their lifecycles exhibit intentionality, emergent patterns of growth, replication, and

10 Ibid., 1225.
11 Ibid., 1224.
12 *Smith v. Schwarzenegger* (n 4).
13 Ibid., 35.
14 David Ferry, 'How the Government Put Tens of Thousands of People at Risk of a Deadly Disease' (*Mother Jones*, 2015) <https://www.motherjones.com/environment/2015/01/valley-fever-california-central-valley-prison/> accessed 27 June 2024.
15 *Smith v. Schwarzenegger* (n 4).
16 *Jackson v. Brown* (n 3) 27.

persistence. These behaviours are not separate and distinct from human systems, but rather pulse through the same social, political, economic, and legal networks that structure the Central Valley.

Cocci Vibrancy and Pathogenic Encounters

Valley Fever is said to be caused by the inhalation of Cocci sporesthat have become airborne. In the United States, Cocci-human contact zones have been mapped across 26 different states.[17] Infection rates and disease prevalence seem to be highest in the desert Southwest and have become a serious public health concern in the San Joaquin region of California's Central Valley.[18] While there is archaeological evidence to suggest that Cocci have co-existed with human and animal communities for millennia, mostly unnoticed,[19] in the past century, changes in the Central Valley's ecology have recalibrated these relational dynamics and have exposed these once subterranean fungal networks to above-ground politics. Amid these newly emergent conditions, Cocci have undergone a profound metabolic transformation.[20] No longer passive inhabitants of soil, these organisms now operate as lively airborne provocateurs, capable of transforming the sociomaterial terrains of the beings and environments they encounter.

Fungal Ecologies and Cocci Life

Cocci begin their existence as soil-bound moulds, organised into large vegetative networks of thread-like filaments (hyphae) that weave together to create the mycelial meshwork sustaining fungal life. These intricate, microscopic, vegetal webs expand in soils that are moist and proliferate as filamentous colonies.[21] In California's Central Valley the sources of this moisture are more-than-natural. While seasonal rainfall provides periodic saturation, the Valley's watery substratum has also been enabled by a long history of infrastructural interventions. From the poorly constructed levee systems of the

17 Samuel D Yoo and others, 'Disseminated Coccidioidomycosis in Africa' (2020) 7 European Journal of Case Reports in Internal Medicine 001659.

18 S Benson Werner and Demosthenes Pappagianis, 'Coccidioidomycosis in Northern California—an Outbreak among Archeology Students near Red Bluff' (1973) 119 California Medicine 16.

19 TN Kirkland and J Fierer, 'Coccidioidomycosis: A Reemerging Infectious Disease' (1996) 2 Emerging Infectious Diseases 192, 192; DH Temple, 'A Possible Case of Coccidioidomycosis from the Los Muertos Site, Tempe, Arizona' (2006) 16 International Journal of Osteoarchaeology 316, 317; Willard Morrow, 'Holocene Coccidioidomycosis: Valley Fever in Early Holocene Bison (Bison Antiquus)' (2006) 98 Mycologia 669.

20 Orion Z McCotter and others, 'Update on the Epidemiology of Coccidioidomycosis in the United States' (2019) 57 Medical Mycology S30, S33.

21 Temple (n 19) 316.

nineteenth century which were prone to failure,[22] to the Valley's heavy reliance on low-cost flood irrigation during the agricultural boom of the twentieth century,[23] the Central Valley's soils have been continuously doused by water that seemed, at least at the time, abundant and limitless. California's agricultural industry has thrived on account of the massive irrigation systems diverting river-waters to farmland, the overuse of phosphorus-laden fertilisers, and the largescale tilling and conversion of its grasslands. But this productivity has come at a steep ecological cost, contributing to water scarcity, droughts, land subsidence, soil degradation, wetland destruction, and deteriorating air quality.[24]

Within these chemically saturated, salinised soils, Cocci colonies, in particular, find an ideal substrate. As salt-tolerant, phosphorus-dependent organisms, capable of enduring wide pH fluctuations,[25] Cocci thrive in agricultural soils when others might perish. In their saprobic state, these organisms participate in the slow metabolisms of decomposition – happily living off the dead matter in their midst, expanding and growing with each rainfall. In mycelial form, as soil-bound decomposers, Cocci remain indifferent to human presence – neither a threat nor an ally. While these moist conditions support Cocci's growth as a mould, the species' ability to thrive, reproduce and spread across vast distances depends on strong climate swings.[26] These deep oscillations - periods of moisture that promote growth punctuated by extreme dry spells - enable the fungus to replicate and disperse. Once rare, these extreme climate shifts are becoming more frequent due to climate change, creating conditions that favour Cocci's expansion into new areas.[27]

22 Peter H Gleick and Elizabeth L Chalecki, 'The Impacts of Climatic Changes for Water Resources of the Colorado and Sacramento-San Joaquin River Basins' (1999) 35 JAWRA Journal of the American Water Resources Association 1429, 1434–5; John Thompson, 'Early Reclamation and Abandonment of the Central Sacramento-San Joaquin Delta' (2006) 6 Sacramento History Journal 41.

23 Donald J Pisani, *From the Family Farm to Agribusiness: The Irrigation Crusade in California and the West, 1850–1931* (University of California Press 2021).

24 Ben Sleeter, 'Late 20th Century Land Change in the Central Valley Ecoregion' (2008) 48 The California Geographer 27; Stephanie S Pincetl, *Transforming California: A Political History of Land Use and Development* (John Hopkins University Press 2003).

25 GH Lacy and FE Swatek, 'Soil Ecology of Coccidioides Immitis at Amerindian Middens in California' (1974) 27 Applied Microbiology 379, 379.

26 Zoya Teirstein, 'Intensifying Atmospheric Rivers Are Leading to a Surge in Valley Fever Cases in California' (*Grist*, 12 February 2024) <https://grist.org/health/intensifying-atmospheric-rivers-are-leading-to-a-surge-in-valley-fever-cases-in-california/> accessed 29 August 2025.

27 Benjamin J Park and others, 'An Epidemic of Coccidioidomycosis in Arizona Associated with Climatic Changes, 1998–2001' (2005) 191 The Journal of Infectious Diseases 1981.

In extreme heat and drought, Cocci colonies transform: their moisture-dependent networks disassemble into thousands of single-celled spores.[28] Cocci do not passively endure stress; they sense, signal, and creatively transform in response to it. Their vast subterranean network, once essential to the organism's survival underground,[29] chemically orchestrates its own fragmentation in response to increasing aridity and thermal force. Cast into dust, the spores await activation by wind, water, animals, or human activity.[30] In this airborne phase, the likelihood of Cocci-human interaction and infection becomes more likely.

When immersed in human terrains – dense with heat, fluids, and immunological armies – Cocci become cunning shapeshifters. They survive and replicate through chemical reconfigurations that allow them to behave less like moulds and more like yeasts.[31] Inhaled spores transform into thick-walled spherules that undergo rapid internal budding[32] and, when full, rupture to release hundreds of new endospores, ready to repeat the cycle without end.[33] To survive in human tissue, Cocci spherules unleash enzymes to suppress human immunological cells, and allow the organism to evade detection.[34] The genetic activity of Cocci during this stage shows an organism under immense stress, a responsive lifeform that is busy upregulating those genes necessary for energy production and maintaining internal stability.[35] In this form, Cocci integrate into the human body so deeply that the body's immune system can no longer distinguish between self and invader.[36] Yet, they retain their own identity, eventually re-emerging as harmless, soil-dwelling mycelia in the decomposing remains of their deceased hosts.[37] Here, one could argue that the organism's pathogenicity is less a fixed identity or inherent quality than a temporary state of relational intensity. In this assemblage, the conceptual

28 Korine N Kolivras and Andrew C Comrie, 'Modeling Valley Fever (Coccidioidomycosis) Incidence on the Basis of Climate Conditions' (2003) 47 International Journal of Biometeorology 87, 88.
29 Merlin Sheldrake, *Entangled Life: How Fungi Make Our Worlds, Change Our Minds, and Shape Our Futures* (Vintage 2021) 57.
30 Kolivras and Comrie (n 28) 88.
31 Michael A Saubolle, Peter P McKellar and Den Sussland, 'Epidemiologic, Clinical, and Diagnostic Aspects of Coccidioidomycosis' (2007) 45 Journal of Clinical Microbiology 26.
32 Garry T Cole and others, 'Factors Regulating Morphogenesis in Coccidioides Immitis' in Hugo Vanden Bossche, Frank C Odds and David Kerridge (eds), *Dimorphic Fungi in Biology and Medicine* (Springer 1993), 191–212.
33 Hirschmann (n 1) 1202.
34 Marley C Caballero Van Dyke and others, 'The Rise of Coccidioides: Forces Against the Dust Devil Unleashed' (2019) 10 Frontiers in Immunology 3–4.
35 Emily Whiston and others, 'Comparative Transcriptomics of the Saprobic and Parasitic Growth Phases in Coccidioides Spp' (2012) 7 PLoS ONE e41034, 2.
36 Natalia Castro-Lopez and Chiung-Yu Hung, 'Immune Response to Coccidioidomycosis and the Development of a Vaccine' (2017) 5 Microorganisms 13, 15.
37 John W Taylor and Bridget M Barker, 'The Endozoan, Small-Mammal Reservoir Hypothesis and the Life Cycle of Coccidioides Species' (2019) 57 Medical Mycology S16.

boundaries between vulnerable (human) bodies and hostile (fungal) ecologies are immediately blurred.

Cocci are social creatures, materially and culturally reconfigured by their encounters. While they regularly use human and animal bodies as dispersal agents and their carcasses as reservoirs during their lifecycle,[38] genomic analyses of mycelia recovered from buried remains suggest that these organisms retain a biological memory of their prior parasitic encounters. This memory directs more of the organism's genetic expression to surviving host-infection than functioning as a free-living saprobe.[39] One could even say that these epigenomic shifts towards stress resistance, cell-wall remodelling and immune evasion are microbial expressions of trauma, and in this particular fungus, they produce distinct sub-populations of the species associated with Valley Fever.[40] Cocci's encounter with humans produces fundamental cellular-level changes in these organisms, changes that remain even after the organism returns to its saprobic state.

In assemblage with human bodies, Cocci become something very different from merely aerosolised fungi. Creative and responsive, they constitute new lifeforms with novel potential. Cocci pathogenicity is thus emergent with its environment. It is lured into being by climatic intensities, soil chemistry, and multispecies entanglement. Its infectious potential is not an intrinsic trait, but an adaptive strategy to help it cope in new environments, and its virulence is itself a protective mechanism to help it persist and replicate.

There is no doubt that Cocci operate as vibrant actants, animated by a kind of ecological responsiveness. Yet, acknowledging this liveliness is not the same as asserting that it should inform frameworks of legal or political accountability. One could argue that this fungus' pathogenic force has been intensified by human agricultural activity, but this does not necessarily unsettle the claim that its presence in the Central Valley remains a natural phenomenon, both inescapable and inevitable. In the following sections, I examine the organism's heightened presence in the San Joaquin Valley as a sociomaterial phenomenon shaped by the dust politics of American expansionism in the Plains and by prevailing knowledge systems around immunity and endemicity. This ecological reading of Valley Fever foregrounds the disease as a microcosm of Empire, a manifestation of exploitative systems and structural inequalities that link vulnerable bodies across time and space.

38 María del Rocío Reyes-Montes and others, 'The Habitat of Coccidioides Spp. and the Role of Animals as Reservoirs and Disseminators in Nature' (2016) 16 BMC Infectious Diseases 550.

39 Nicholas P Money, *Fungi: A Short Introduction* (OUP 2016) 13.

40 Thomas J Sharpton and others, 'Comparative Genomic Analyses of the Human Fungal Pathogens *Coccidioides* and Their Relatives' (2009) 19 Genome Research 1722; Daniel R Kollath, Karis J Miller and Bridget M Barker, 'The Mysterious Desert Dwellers: Coccidioides Immitis and Coccidioides Posadasii, Causative Fungal Agents of Coccidioidomycosis' (2019) 10 Virulence 222, 223.

The Dust-History of Cocci

Just over 1,000 miles east of California's Central Valley lie the Southern Plains of the United States, a region encompassing parts of Texas, Oklahoma, Kansas, Colorado, and New Mexico. For centuries these lands sustained Indigenous peoples including the Navajo, Comanche, and Apache nations, as well as Pueblo communities who migrated and settled throughout the area during the eighteenth and nineteenth centuries. However, during the upheaval of the American Civil War, and as the government set its sights westward, these long-settled communities were violently dispossessed of their lands, and many Indigenous nations were forcibly pushed onto reservations in different states.[41] Once emptied of their native communities, the Plains were declared "open" for white settlement under the Homestead Act of 1862, and by 1901, promises of private ownership were being readily exchanged for settler occupation and cultivation.[42]

In the decades that followed, settlers arrived in waves, urged on by government policy and the allure of new opportunity. Buying into the myth of western prosperity, they ploughed and tilled the land for profit, with little concern for the native fauna that long held its soils in place. As Worster observes, when the settlers arrived in the Plains they came upon an "ancient set of alliances" where "all living things needed each other, depended on each other, to withstand the harsher side of climate".[43] Yet, in the few intervening years of American colonialism, the region experienced more sudden and profound ecological change than it had in the preceding 40,000 years,[44] and much of that has been attributed to widespread settler ignorance about how to work *with* the land and its climate, rather than to try and control it.[45]

Land degradation has been described as a defining feature of imperial expansion, colonial agricultural policies, and western farming practices around the world.[46] The introduction of industrial agriculture in the Southern Plains was no different. During the early periods of American expansionism,

41 Sherry Lynn Smith, *The Future of the Southern Plains* (University of Oklahoma Press 2003) 4–8.

42 Hannah Holleman, *Dust Bowls of Empire: Imperialism, Environmental Politics, and the Injustice of 'Green' Capitalism* (Yale University Press 2018) 55–7.

43 Donald Worster, *Dust Bowl: The Southern Plains in the 1930s* (Oxford University Press 2004) 66.

44 Ibid., 78.

45 Gilbert C Fite, 'Great Plains Farming: A Century of Change and Adjustment' (1977) 51 Agricultural History 244.

46 Piers Blaikie and Harold Brookfield, 'Colonialism, Development and Degradation' in Piers Blaikie and Harold Brookfield (eds) *Land Degradation and Society* (Routledge 1987); Douglas Southgate, 'The Causes of Land Degradation along "Spontaneously" Expanding Agricultural Frontiers in the Third World' (1990) 66 Land Economics 93; David Anderson, 'Depression, Dust Bowl, Demography, and Drought: The Colonial State and Soil Conservation in East Africa during the 1930s' (1984) 83 African Affairs 321.

the commodification of land stripped the region's soils of essential nutrients and exposed it to wind and water erosion.[47] In the Southern Plains, what had once been a complex, resilient ecosystem was rapidly turned into an extractive agricultural zone. This phase of legal and territorial expansion was not just incidental, but central to the project of American settler colonialism. Technological innovations enabled a shift from subsistence farming to large-scale surplus production, aligning with federal ambitions for economic growth and territorial consolidation. By the early twentieth century, agricultural output across the Plains had surged – a trend that only accelerated during the First World War, when wheat cultivation doubled in parts of the region.[48]

But the benefits of this agricultural boom were short-lived. After the end of the War, as European farmers resumed production, crop prices in the United States collapsed. Burdened by debt from years of drought and the rising costs of mechanisation, American farmers expanded onto marginal lands,[49] relied heavily on tractor and combine technology, and abandoned soil conservation practices in a desperate effort to stay profitable.[50] Over time, prolonged drought, falling crop prices, and industrial pressures drove many small family farms and individual homesteads out of business, clearing the way for large farming corporations backed by federal policies promoting more "efficient" and sustainable agriculture.[51] Fuelled by a desire for territorial expansion and national agricultural development, the colonisation of the Southern Plains proceeded with minimal environmental regulation.

According to Harden and Hyman, while human agricultural practice is "strongly affected by the physical attributes of place – soil, water, climate, biota, and topography", it is also a highly intrusive practice that inscribes its violence directly onto the land by altering its underlying chemical and biological processes.[52] In the Southern Plains, intensive farming and overgrazing stripped away the fertile layer of topsoil, exposing the land to wind and water erosion. These effects were intensified by shifting precipitation patterns and changes in Atlantic and Pacific sea surface temperatures, which together triggered a series of droughts across the region. The dry, unanchored soil was then swept up by powerful winds and carried for miles, forming the dark and imposing dust storms that would come to define this era in American memory.

47 Holleman (n 42) 62.

48 Gilbert C Fite, 'The Great Plains: A Colonial Area' (1961) 40 Current History 280, 281.

49 Ibid.

50 George S Wehrwein, 'A Land Policy as a Part of an Agricultural Program' (1925) 7 Journal of Farm Economics 289, 294–5.

51 'The History of Public Lands Grazing' (*Western Watersheds Project*) <https://westernwatersheds.org/the-history-of-public-lands-grazing/> accessed 11 July 2025; Fite (n 45) 252.

52 Carol P Harden and Glenn G Hyman, 'Agriculture and Soil Erosion' in Carol P Harden and Glenn G Hyman, *The Physical Geography of South America* (Oxford University Press 2007) 289.

In this way, the land – reshaped by human intervention – became both a witness to, and an agent of, environmental collapse.

The cultivation of the Plains reflects a deep and intimate connection between the destruction of ecosystems and the destruction of societies. As Holleman notes, the "ruling capitalist ethos" of the time cannot be easily "disentangled from the white supremacist logic driving and legitimising the domination of indigenous peoples, as well as the expropriation and domination of their land".[53] This profit-driven individualistic mindset permeated many of the agricultural practices of that time. As Morris states, "in a frenzy of farm colonisation, thousands of mechanised agrarians helped themselves to the topsoil with as much zeal as the hard-pressed ranchers had plundered the grass".[54] In states like Texas, expansive property rights allowed landowners to deplete underground aquifers without regard for collective or ecological impact. Guided by a rationalist man-over-nature worldview, many settlers were of the belief that cultivation could reshape the harsh climate of the Southern Plains, and famously asserted that "rainfall followed the plough".[55] One could argue that this worldview was encouraged by policies that continued to prioritise private ownership and economic growth over environmental sustainability and ecological knowledge,[56] even once state agencies realised the environmental costs of overgrazing and agricultural overdevelopment.[57] In the end, the land, once moist and fertile, now barren dust, was left to bear the consequences.

Beginning in the 1930s, a series of severe and prolonged dust storms led to the Southern Plains being labelled the "Dust Bowl", a name that captured nearly a decade of environmental devastation. Although extended drought is often blamed, the severity of these dust storms was greatly worsened by soil erosion caused by industrialised agriculture –sustained through by corporate farming, mechanised production, and the support of government subsidies.[58] By 1934, it was estimated that 65 percent of the Great Plains' lands had been damaged by wind erosion.[59] Far from being local disturbances, these dust storms became continental events. Over 12 million tonnes of the Plains' soil was displaced, carried eastward, and deposited as far away as New York City and

53 Holleman (n 42) 66.

54 John Miller Morris, 'When Corporations Rule the Llano Estacado: The Glorious Past and Uncertain Future of the Southern High Plains Family Farm' in Sherry Lynn Smith (ed), *The Future of the Southern Plains* (University of Oklahoma Press 2003) 48.

55 Fite (n 48).

56 Worster (n 43) 4.

57 Wehrwein (n 50).

58 John Borchert, 'The Dust Bowl in the 1970s' (1971) 61 Annals of the Association of American Geographers 1.

59 David M Cutler, Grant Miller and Douglas M Norton, 'Evidence on Early-Life Income and Late-Life Health from America's Dust Bowl Era' (2007) 104 Proceedings of the National Academy of Sciences 13244.

the Atlantic Ocean. On "Black Sunday", the term used to describe one of the most catastrophic dust storms to have been recorded, the scene in many parts of the region resembled a setting from a sci-fi thriller. The sky turned electric, radios cut out, ignitions failed, and waves of sand rolled across the roads like ocean swells, causing cars to veer into ditches and trains to derail.[60] As Egan describes, Black Sunday was an apocalyptic collision of nature and human design.[61]

Mobile Dusts and Migrating Bodies

The Dust Bowl era was marked not only by the movement of soil, but also the mass displacement of people. Between 1934 and 1935, during the height of the dust storms, approximately 250,000 agricultural workers left the Southern Plains for California's Central Valley in search of more stable living and working conditions.[62] In some counties, population losses reached 50 to 70 percent.[63] By comparison, California presented a strikingly different agricultural landscape. In the San Joaquin Valley, farmland had quadrupled by the early 1930s, and restrictive immigration policies and mass deportation of Mexican workers created a significant shortage of labour. To fill this gap, cotton growers in California actively recruited displaced farmers from Oklahoma and Texas by promising rail fares and offering wages up to 50 percent higher than those available back home.[64]

Many of the settlers migrating from the Plains to the Central Valley came from lower socioeconomic backgrounds and had limited exposure to modern amenities such as electricity and indoor plumbing.[65] As the number of migrants quickly outpaced available jobs, many Dust Bowl refugees fell into

60 Timothy Egan, *The Worst Hard Time* (Mariner Classics 2006) 7.

61 Egan (n 60).

62 Jason Long and Henry E Siu, 'Refugees From Dust and Shrinking Land: Tracking the Dust Bowl Migrants' (National Bureau of Economic Research, March 2016) <https://www.nber.org/papers/w22108> accessed 14 January 2025; Robert A McLeman and others, 'What We Learned from the Dust Bowl: Lessons in Science, Policy, and Adaptation' (2014) 35 Population and Environment 417, 7–8; State of California, 'The Dust Bowl, California, and the Politics of Hard Times' (*California State Capitol Museum*) <https://capitolmuseum.ca.gov/exhibits/the-dust-bowl-california-and-the-politics-of-hard-times/> accessed 14 January 2025.

63 Elliott West, 'Trails and Footprints: The Past of the Future Southern Plains' in Sherry Lynn Smith (ed), *The Future of the Southern Plains* (University of Oklahoma Press 2003) 18.

64 State of California, 'The Dust Bowl, California, and the Politics of Hard Times' (*California State Capitol Museum*) <https://capitolmuseum.ca.gov/experiences/exhibits/the-dust-bowl-california-and-the-politics-of-hard-times/> accessed 6 October 2025.

65 James N Gregory, *American Exodus: The Dust Bowl Migration and Okie Culture in California* (Oxford University Press 1989) 10; Robin A Fanslow, 'The Migrant Experience | Articles and Essays | Voices from the Dust Bowl: The Charles L. Todd and Robert Sonkin Migrant Worker Collection, 1940-1941 | Digital Collections | Library of Congress' (*Library of Congress, Washington, D.C. 20540 USA*) <https://www.loc.gov/collections/todd-and-sonkin-migrant-workers-from-1940-to-1941/articles-and-essays/the-migrant-experience/> accessed 14 January 2025.

extreme poverty. Popularly known as "Okies", these families often lived in makeshift camps, along roadsides, in fields, and near irrigation ditches, with little access to food, shelter, or sanitation.[66] They were frequently met with suspicion and hostility from local residents who viewed them as uneducated, dishonest, and incompatible with California's modern way of life.[67]

As Manzella notes, the Dust Bowl migrations reveal the deep entanglement between citizenship, race, and land. While white settlers from the Plains made up the largest group of internal migrants during this period, their displacement exposed what she calls the "myths of possession" at the heart of settler society – the belief that land ownership guarantees power, prosperity, and belonging. These myths not only justified expansionist policies but also encouraged extractive and unsustainable farming practices that ultimately eroded the very livelihoods they were meant to secure. The agricultural system thus itself became a mechanism of displacement. Rather than ensuring autonomy and economic independence, it transformed landowning farmers into landless labourers. This dispossession was reinforced at multiple levels by corporate farmers, local officials, state representatives, and federal authorities through restrictive migrant laws, exploitative labour practices, and inadequate housing and sanitation. These structural forces worked to undermine the migrants' claim to full citizenship, casting suspicion on their very "American-ness".[68] In this way, the promises of industrial agriculture and capitalist expansion proved hollow, uprooting a quarter of a million people and relocating them to lands that, while more fertile, remained culturally inhospitable.

In the immediate aftermath of the Dust Bowl migrations, California recorded its first significant rise in cases of what was then termed "desert fever". This surge signalled more than a public health anomaly; it revealed a convergence of ecological disruption, labour displacement, and structural inequality. A national study mapping Valley Fever outbreaks from 1940 onwards found that nearly one-third of all cases recorded between 1940 and 1949 occurred in California.[69] Yet, the fungus causing the disease was not confined to California alone – clinical and archaeological data collected from the Dust Bowl suggest that Cocci might also have been endemic to the Plains region.[70] The spike in disease rates in the Valley could

66 California (n 62).

67 Thaithao Nguyen, 'The Dust Bowl Migration: Fear, Discrimination, Exclusion' (2018) 5 The Toro Historical Review.

68 Abigail GH Manzella, *Migrating Fictions: Gender, Race, and Citizenship in U.S. Internal Displacements* (Ohio State University Press 2018) 70–1.

69 Michael Freedman and others, 'Coccidioidomycosis Outbreaks, United States and Worldwide, 1940–2015' (2018) 24 Emerging Infectious Diseases 417.

70 Morgan E Gorris and others, 'Expansion of Coccidioidomycosis Endemic Regions in the United States in Response to Climate Change' (2019) 3 GeoHealth 308, 322; Morgan E Gorris and others, 'Advocating for Coccidioidomycosis to Be a Reportable Disease Nationwide in the United

not simply be attributed to the natural presence of Cocci; there was something going on that was conditioning the virulence of this relationship in this part of the country.

Multiple factors may have contributed to the rise in Valley Fever cases in California during this period. Intensified dust storms, propelled by both climatic extremes, capitalist extractivism, and agricultural mismanagement, may have carried Cocci-laden soils from the Plains, across great distances, to expose new populations to the pathogen. At the same time, even if they had arrived free from infection, many Dust Bowl migrants were now living in makeshift camps on bare, undisturbed land, creating disruptions that may have exposed them to infection. Given Cocci's capacity to persist dormant in human tissue and reactivate under conditions of immunosuppression and stress, it is also plausible that some of these migrants may have arrived with a past history of asymptomatic infection, with the disease now manifesting under the strain of post-migration life. The fact that most cases of Valley Fever, up to 60 percent according to some estimates,[71] are *a*symptomatic, with infections often resolving on their own, it should be alarming that so many residents of the Valley were manifesting symptoms serious enough to prompt a public health inquiry.

Now one could, as the courts have explained in relation to prisoners, attribute this simply to a biological predisposition – some bodies are *genetically* more prone to the disease. One could even relate the high rates of disease to the migration and settlement of a large population of immunologically naïve people from not only the Dust Bowl region, but also from outside of the United States, many of whom became agricultural labourers and were thus exposed to Cocci as an occupational hazard.[72] While this may explain the high rates of infection amongst racial and ethnic minorities during this period of American history, it does not explain why this susceptibility to disease has carried forward into future generations. Valley Fever is not a hereditary condition in the genetic sense; Cocci spores do not inscribe themselves onto a host's DNA. Yet the susceptibility of later generations suggests that inheritance may take other forms.

Frost has eloquently argued that even our molecular structure, the very basic building blocks that enable genetic-level functioning, are not inherent, but socially contingent. While we may have been born with a particular genetic "blueprint", whether those genes express themselves – manifest in

States and Encouraging Disease Surveillance across North and South America' (2023) 9 Journal of Fungi 83.

71 Amy P Hsu, 'The Known and Unknown "Knowns" of Human Susceptibility to Coccidioidomycosis' (2024) 10 Journal of Fungi 257.

72 Ibid., 269.

disease, for instance – may depend on environmental factors.[73] This view is supported by a Valley Fever study undertaken by Harrison, who notes that conventional narratives of infectious disease imagine a tidy evolutionary pattern, where pathogen infects a host, antibodies come to its defence and, over successive generations, the host-genotype which confers resistance ends up being passed down to descendants. In this story, the host-parasite relation gradually stabilises, either through the host's enhanced immunological resilience or through the parasite's reduction in virulence. Yet Cocci resist this evolutionary script.

Molecular and chemical analyses of Cocci spores recovered from the 750-year-old skeletal remains of a Native American individual in an endemic zone in Arizona revealed that the organism's composition has changed very little over the past seven centuries.[74] The fungus persists with remarkable consistency, indifferent to human expectations of evolutionary compromise. Fungal adaptation cannot explain why Native Americans, who have resided in endemic zones for millennia, demonstrate a greater susceptibility to Valley Fever than newly arriving populations.[75] In addition to higher infection risk, Native American individuals are also more likely than any other social group to contract disseminated disease and have the highest rates of disease-related mortality.[76] If Valley Fever were only a matter of host genetics, antibodies, and evolutionary selection, this story would have resolved long ago. Immunity, in this sense, cannot be understood as a purely biological inheritance. According to Harrison, susceptibility to disease is not a natural failure of certain bodies, but the patterned outcome of environment, politics, and fungal agency entwined.

Harrison, along with a broader constellation of epigenetic researchers, believes that genomic expression is not a self-contained biological script but an open-ended dialogue with sociomaterial worlds. The lived conditions of oppressed communities, entangled in histories of extraction, discrimination, structural abandonment, and limited access to socioeconomic resources, cannot be processed through genetic determinism alone. The overrepresentation of coronary heart disease, hypertension, and diabetes among racial minorities are not merely biological events but symptoms

73 Samantha Frost, 'The Attentive Body: How the Indexicality of Epigenetic Processes Enriches Our Understanding of Embodied Subjectivity' (2020) 26 Body & Society 3.

74 William R Harrison, 'Dangerous Dirt: Paleopathology of Valley Fever and the Biopolitics of Race' in *The Anthropology of Infectious Disease* (Routledge 1997) 86–7.

75 Heather L Mead and others, 'Coccidioidomycosis in Northern Arizona: An Investigation of the Host, Pathogen, and Environment Using a Disease Triangle Approach' (2022) 7 mSphere e00352.

76 Orion McCotter and others, 'Coccidioidomycosis Among American Indians and Alaska Natives, 2001–2014' (2019) 6 Open Forum Infectious Diseases ofz052, 5–7.

of systemic exposure to uneven geographies of care, to environmental toxicity, to the slow violence of racialised neglect, and to white settler colonial trauma.[77]

Like fungal bodies under stress, finding ways to survive inhospitable environments, human bodies must also develop adaptive, often precarious, strategies of persistence.[78] For epigeneticists, racial difference and class inequality thus become active participants in the shaping of life chances on a *material* level. In the face of isolation, physical and financial insecurity, malnutrition, and exposure to environmental toxins, bodies upregulate the hormones, neurotransmitters, and proteins they need to survive these hostile conditions (e.g. cortisol, adrenaline, endorphins) and downregulate those chemicals that are not essential to immediate survival. These alterations to the body's chemistry can suppress the immune pathways critical for defence against foreign pathogens, leaving the body more vulnerable to diseases that thrive within weakened immune systems, and produce profound imbalances in who contracts and who dies from infection.[79] Moreover, fungal and viral pathogens are not entirely silent participants in these exchanges between gene and social environment. They, too, are capable of altering the epigenetic landscape of host immune cells to facilitate their own growth and replication.[80]

Perhaps most interestingly, the biological effects of these environmental pressures do not end with the bodies that directly endure them. Folded into the epigenetic structure, the chemical changes and relations that these pressures enable become heritable. Their molecular traces ripple forward, carried as epigenetic inscriptions that can echo across generations.[81] These inscriptions

77 Zaneta M Thayer and Christopher W Kuzawa, 'Biological Memories of Past Environments: Epigenetic Pathways to Health Disparities' (2011) 6 Epigenetics 798; Jennifer W Robinette and Jennifer A Smith, 'Accelerated Molecular Aging in Socioeconomically Disadvantaged Neighborhoods: A Racial/Ethnic Comparison' (2025) 93 Health & Place 103446; Kat Chief Moon-Riley and others, 'The Biological Impacts of Indigenous Residential School Attendance on the next Generation' (2019) 7 SSM - Population Health 100343; Connie J Mulligan, 'Systemic Racism Can Get under Our Skin and into Our Genes' (2021) 175 American Journal of Physical Anthropology 399.

78 Frost (n 73).

79 Saeed Aslani and others, 'Epigenetic Alterations Underlying Autoimmune Diseases' (2016) 49 Autoimmunity 69; Anura Hewagama and Bruce Richardson, 'The Genetics and Epigenetics of Autoimmune Diseases' (2009) 33 Journal of Autoimmunity 3; Belinda L Needham and others, 'Life Course Socioeconomic Status and DNA Methylation in Genes Related to Stress Reactivity and Inflammation: The Multi-Ethnic Study of Atherosclerosis' (2015) 10 Epigenetics 958; Jeffrey D Jenks and others, 'Race and Ethnicity: Risk Factors for Fungal Infections?' (2023) 19 PLOS Pathogens 1.

80 Smita Kulkarni and others, 'Editorial: Epigenetics of Infectious Diseases' (2022) 13 Frontiers in Immunology; Dylan Wrede and others, 'Pulmonary Pathogen-Induced Epigenetic Modifications' (2023) 7 Epigenomes 13.

81 Bastiaan T Heijmans and others, 'Persistent Epigenetic Differences Associated with Prenatal Exposure to Famine in Humans' (2008) 105 Proceedings of the National Academy of Sciences 17046.

can modulate genomic expression in future bodies – bodies that have yet to endure those environmental pressures directly – silencing, activating, or reconfiguring genes tied to immunity, disease susceptibility, and survival. Consequently, environmental perturbations have trans-corporeal effects; they move beyond the bodily boundaries of the physically exposed individual. Bodies retain traces of generational trauma within their cellular and molecular architectures, even when these pressurised conditions no longer exist. These inscriptions lie dormant in our cellular machinery, awaiting reactivation, not unlike Cocci's spherulation potential.

As Harrison remarks, when racial difference is attributed to genetic factors, rac*ism* becomes normalised. It is then possible to become so fixated on biological race as *the* defining factor of social difference (in rates of Valley Fever infection, for example), that other socioeconomic and political factors, factors that we *can do* something about, factors that can be linked to social inequities and cultural oppression, disappear from view. While many of us may possess a vulnerability to disease as "risk factors" embedded in our genes, whether they are expressed or not, and the effects they give rise to, are dependent on our social, physical, and perceptual environment.[82] Krieger's ecosocial theory of disease refers to this as a form of "embodied inequality".[83] As Walton explains "[g]enes are not about fate. They are about potentials and possibilities within particular contexts".[84] While there is no shortage of scholarship that speaks about the effects of social inequality on the mental well-being of those experiencing it, we remain largely resistant to the idea that social inequality can generate physiological changes in the bodies of oppressed persons, and may be capable of igniting otherwise dormant risk factors.

Nevertheless, to search for a singular or even definitive cause of the Valley Fever epidemic during the Dust Bowl era and beyond is to overlook the entangled agencies at work and, to some extent, impose temporal and geographic limits on a phenomenon that is much wider in scale and effect. What is needed is wider recognition of the nature-culture ontology of this phenomenon. Cocci do not merely infect; they follow, they wait, they circulate through bodies, air, and soil. Their movements are driven equally by cultural practice and human politics as they are by climate and soil. Bodies – human, microbial, geological, hydrological, atmospheric – are not just passive containers but forces and

82 Kristien Hens and Leni Van Goidsenhoven, 'Autism, Genetics and Epigenetics: Why the Lived Experience Matters in Research' (2017) 4 BioNews, December.

83 Nancy Krieger, 'Methods for the Scientific Study of Discrimination and Health: An Ecosocial Approach' (2012) 102 American Journal of Public Health 936.

84 Jamie Stephen Walton, 'Fit in Your Genes: An Introduction to Genes and Epigenetics for Forensic Practitioners' (2021) The Journal of Forensic Practice 193, 189–200.

vectors, transporting illness and death across territories, generations,[85] and even geological epochs,[86] creating zones of risk where previously there were none. Given what we know about how Cocci live and adapt, how they are capable of reestablishing themselves as networks of hyphae in the remains of their host, it is likely that the Dust Bowl migrations and the accompanying high rates of disease contributed to the Valley later becoming a "hyperendemic" zone for the fungus. The idea that bodies operate as transporters of fungal activity is supported by studies which suggest that the presence of Cocci in previously non-endemic regions may have been triggered by the migration and burial of infected animals and people from endemic sites.[87] Consequently, the Valley's emergence as a hyperendemic zone in the contemporary moment is not just a natural consequence of fungal presence but an artefact of Nature's collisions with human politics. The emergence of disease is an effect of these convergences , and its prevalence amongst certain social groups is not a matter of *just* biological susceptibility, but an expression of structural inequality.

In considering these movements I do not wish to collapse relationality into causality. Rather, I want to open up space for thinking otherwise, about how disease emerges not from isolated agents and events but from dynamic assemblages of climate, capital, soil, species, and politics over time and across geographic boundaries. At the outset of *Exposed*, Alaimo insists that "the Anthropocene is no time for transcendent, definitive mappings, transparent knowledge systems or confident epistemologies".[88] What this epoch demands are "trans-corporeal mappings of networks of risk, harm, culpability, and responsibility" that flow through bodies, infrastructures, ecologies, implicating even the most "ordinary" denizens.[89] The Dust Bowl was not simply a human disaster but a multispecies event, the effects of which are still felt by contemporary populations placed under conditions of deep stress. The settler logics of possession and extraction, intensified by the volatility of climate, contributed materially to the transformation of the Valley into a hyperendemic landscape, not solely through policy or migration, but through the ecological re-patterning that such systems of domination inevitably provoke. It is through this lens, adopting varying temporal and geographic scales – from the microscopic to the global, from the embodied to the trans-corporeal, from the Holocene to the Anthropocene – that our legal response to Valley Fever in the prison must be rethought.

85 David M Engelthaler, James C Chatters and Arturo Casadevall, 'Was Coccidioides a Pre-Columbian Hitchhiker to Southcentral Washington?' (2023) 14 mBio <https://journals.asm.org/doi/10.1128/mbio.00232-23> accessed 10 July 2025.

86 Morrow (n 19).

87 Engelthaler, Chatters and Casadevall (n 85).

88 Stacy Alaimo, *Exposed* (University of Minnesota Press 2016) 3.

89 Ibid.

The Institutional Response to Prisoner Disease

I want to return now to the issue of Valley Fever in the prison and to examine how the California Department of Corrections has sought to alleviate the prevalence of disease amongst prisoners. Many of the policies that it has implemented treat Valley Fever as a biomedical problem, confronted by inherently vulnerable inmates. This framing of prisoner disease, and the patterns of practice established on its basis, ignores the wider ecological and structural causes of infection, illness, and death. In overlooking the broader ecological and structural forces that shape disease in prisons, legal and institutional responses to Valley Fever frame it as a matter of public health rather than a form of environmental injustice.

In the earlier sections of this chapter, I explained how the courts have construed the San Joaquin region as a hyperendemic zone where Valley-fever-causing fungi are "naturally occurring". While I have sought to disrupt this characterisation of the fungus as a passive and static pathogen and its habitat as a natural reservoir, it is undeniable that juridical narratives exert an extraordinary degree of power in organising our world and conditioning the interactions we have with it.[90] For example, when the courts describe the "conditions of confinement" as issues that can be tied solely to institutional experiences of the prison, they simultaneously render everything beyond those physical boundaries irrelevant to legal consideration. We lose sight of the fact that prisons are not isolated infrastructures. They are embedded in their surrounding ecology.

The power of legal narratives is further enhanced when their interpretations of reality are connected to "science". In Chapter 2, I explained the authority that science wields in western thought, with its visions of human exceptionalism and the value of empirical inquiry. But the world that science and law imagine and deploy through their doctrines, charts, images, graphs and collections of "data", is a world among many. Law and science are "world-making practices" that "tend to make the world they know".[91] Accordingly, they create their own (material and conceptual) objects by ignoring interactions, agencies, relationalities that do not affirm their ideas about how the world is or *should be*. As De La Cadena and Blaser explain "[w]hat the community of knowers does not recognise as knowledge is displaced along with its reality-making possibilities".[92]

The courts' uncritical use of endemicity as an objective marker of Cocci's natural presence in a geographic area reflects the partial and exclusionary

90 David Delaney, *The Spatial, the Legal and the Pragmatics of World-Making* (Routledge 2010).

91 Marisol De La Cadena and Mario Blaser (eds), *A World of Many Worlds* (Duke University Press 2018) 6.

92 Ibid.

reality co-produced by western law and science. In the United States, endemic regions are typically identified in two ways. First, through soil sampling, a costly, hazardous, and unreliable method due to the fungus' uneven distribution and environmental variability.[93] Crucially, soil sampling is often triggered by public health data, meaning it reflects human disease presence rather than the fungus' ecological distribution. As argued earlier, these human-fungal interactions are shaped by natural, social, and political factors.

The second and more common method relies on the collection of epidemiological data, especially skin tests indicating prior exposure. But such testing is guided by reported infections, which are themselves shaped by class and race politics.[94] These tests may reveal past infection, but not where or how exposure occurred. Given that both humans and fungi move, and that Cocci can remain dormant in host bodies for years after exposure,[95] this method also fails to locate the fungus' "natural" home.

Together, these approaches offer limited insight into whether the San Joaquin Valley is truly native Cocci territory, and this is only compounded by research which suggests that regional patterns of disease may be driven more by fungal dispersal than by local fungal growth.[96] In this light, endemicity is not a neutral scientific fact but a relational outcome – produced through multispecies entanglements and political, agricultural, and environmental conditions. Yet courts reinforce the idea that disease simply "belongs" in certain geographies, masking Valley Fever's dynamic, episodic, and mobile nature.

In the carceral context, skin tests are now being performed on inmates housed in Avenal and PVSP to determine whether they have a history of prior exposure and have built up the necessary antibodies to fight off future infection. Inmates who have a positive skin test are deemed "safe" to be housed in prisons located in hyperendemic zones.[97] Yet, we already know from

93 Molly Radosevich and others, 'Characterizing the Soil Microbial Community Associated with the Fungal Pathogen Coccidioides Immitis' (2025) 11 Journal of Fungi 309–10 <https://www.mdpi.com/2309-608X/11/4/309> accessed 6 October 2025.

94 Camille J Saucier and others, 'Overcoming Health Information Inequities: Valley Fever Information Repertoires Among Vulnerable Communities in California' (2024) 39 Health Communication 2793; Alyssa Nguyen, Kristen Knutson and Yanyi Djamba, 'Epidemiologic Summary of Valley Fever (Coccidioidomycosis) in California, 2020-2021' (California Department of Public Health 2021) Surveillance and Statistics Section <https://www.cdph.ca.gov/Programs/CID/DCDC/CDPH%20Document%20Library/CocciEpiSummary2020-2021.pdf> accessed 29 August 2025.

95 Nancy A Chow and others, 'Factors Influencing Distribution of Coccidioides Immitis in Soil, Washington State, 2016' (2021) 6 mSphere e00598.

96 Robert Wagner and others, 'Coccidioides Undetected in Soils from Agricultural Land and Uncorrelated with Time or the Greater Soil Fungal Community on Undeveloped Land' (2023) 19 PLOS Pathogens e1011391.

97 Sarah M Rios, 'Poverty, Prisons, Pollution and Valley Fever' in *Lessons in Environmental Justice: From Civil Rights to Black Lives Matter and Idle No More* (Sage Publications 2021) 199.

Harrison's study that immunological resistance is not an accurate predictor of how the body may respond to infection in new surroundings and under different conditions. Relying on the presence of antibodies as safeguards to disease obscures the role that social environment plays in conditioning immunological resilience. This is supported by research which indicates that skin test results can be ambivalent. The same host can express positive antigen results at one time, and negative at another, suggesting that immunological function may vary with other factors.[98] In how it is being used in Avenal and PVSP, a positive skin test confirms a body that is already damaged by infection, allowing the CDCR to, as Rios observes, "channel the risks created in poisonous places [back onto] powerless people".[99]

The use of skin tests to predict disease resistance also diminishes the agency, creativity and responsiveness of this fungus. Cocci find ways of adapting to life in volatile and hostile conditions. Regional genetic variation in Cocci suggests that its patterns of behaviour are shaped by both the physical and sociopolitical attributes of the environment.[100] Cocci infections are not universal or uniform phenomena; they emerge through situated, place-based relationships between (human and nonhuman) bodies, environments, and infrastructures. This is further supported by research which suggests that human immunity may also be strain-specific and may not extend to all variants of an organism,[101] and may also not protect individuals from disease reactivation under new conditions.[102] The cellular makeup of human and fungal bodies is fundamentally transformed through their encounter, producing new ecological subjectivities capable of acting in novel and unpredictable ways.

The precarity of prison life stems not only from the threat of physical violence, but also from the biological exposures and harms it imposes.[103] One study of African American prisoners identified a strong epigenetic link

98 Edward C Oldfield III and others, 'Prediction of Relapse After Treatment of Coccidioidomycosis' (1997) 25 Clinical Infectious Diseases 1205.

99 Rios (n 97) 200.

100 'Coccidioides Genomes' (*Broad Institute*, 3 June 2015) <https://www.broadinstitute.org/scientific-community/science/projects/fungal-genome-initiative/coccidioides-genomes> accessed 2 October 2025; Mark Voorhies and others, '"Select and Resequence" Methods Enable a Genome-Wide Association Study of the Dimorphic Human Fungal Pathogen Coccidioides Posadasii' (2025) 17 Genome Biology and Evolution evaf135.

101 RA Cox and DM Magee, 'Protective Immunity in Coccidioidomycosis: The Life Cycle and Biology of Coccidioides Immitis' (1998) 149 Research in Immunology 417, 419–20.

102 David Salkin and Armia Said, 'Reinfection with Coccidioidomycosis' (1993) 17 Clinical Infectious Diseases 1066.

103 Michael Massoglia, 'Incarceration as Exposure: The Prison, Infectious Disease, and Other Stress-Related Illnesses' (2008) 49 Journal of Health and Social Behavior 56; Malcolm Coffman, 'The Neurological Imprint of Incarceration and Its Effect on Recidivism' 37 Notre Dame Journal of Law, Ethics & Public Policy 2023; Justin D Strong and others, 'The Body in Isolation: The Physical Health Impacts of Incarceration in Solitary Confinement' (2020) 15 PLOS ONE e0238510; Michael Massoglia and William Alex Pridemore, 'Incarceration and Health' (2015) 41 Annual Review of Sociology 291.

between incarceration and accelerated cellular ageing, suggesting that the chronic stress and insecurity of prison life can produce a "weathering effect" on the body's biological systems,[104] leaving prisoners more susceptible to chronic health problems and disease.[105] Because racial minorities and economically marginalised groups are disproportionately incarcerated, the biological harms of prison life fall most heavily on those already facing structural disadvantage.[106] By focusing narrowly on the biological markers of disease vulnerability, the CDCR overlooks how prison conditions themselves may undermine prisoners' ability to resist disease. Likewise, by relying on endemicity as the main measure of infection risk and ignoring the broader ecological conditions that sustain prisons, the courts effectively normalise the prevalence of illness among incarcerated people in certain regions.

It is important to point out that the CDCR's implementation of an exclusion policy based on skin-testing came on the back of a 2013 District Court order which required it to divert high-risk prisoners from Avenal and PVSP,[107] and a 2015 Supreme Court ruling that found that severe overcrowding in California's prisons violated its inmates' rights to constitutionally adequate medical and mental health care.[108] The CDCR committed millions of dollars to rehousing Black, Filipino, and Native American prisoners in institutions located in non-endemic areas. At the time, Avenal and PVSP were two of the most overcrowded correctional facilities, with Avenal in particular housing double the inmates it was designed to hold.[109] Current CDCR reports indicate that both PVSP and Avenal are still operating at 30 percent over their design capacity.[110]

When assessing the CDCR's liability, the courts dismissed prison overcrowding as irrelevant to Valley Fever on the grounds that the disease is not contagious.[111] However, in so doing, the courts fail to consider how overcrowded conditions intensify prisoners' biological vulnerability to disease. Overcrowding is not just a vector for transmission; it produces environments of compromised immunity, inadequate care, and prolonged exposure to environmental pathogens. Overcrowding also produces conditions which make prison

104 Mark T Berg and others, 'Losing Years Doing Time: Incarceration Exposure and Accelerated Biological Aging among African American Adults' (2021) 62 Journal of health and social behavior 460.

105 Shannon Sullivan, 'Inheriting Racist Disparities in HealthEpigenetics and the Transgenerational Effects of White Racism' (2013) 1 Critical Philosophy of Race 190, 196.

106 Berg and others (n 104).

107 *Plata v Brown* [2013] ND Cal No. 01-cv-01351.

108 *Brown v Plata* (2011) 563 493 (US).

109 Rios (n 97) 320–1.

110 'Weekly Report of Population' (2025) SOMS-TPOP-1 2.

111 *Hines v. Youseff* 914 F.3d 1218 (9th Cir. 2019), 1226.

life more psychologically, physiologically, and immunologically taxing.[112] In environments that are loud, chaotic, lacking privacy, where violence is routinised, and prisoners have little control over their day-to-day well-being, the body's stress response generates certain chemicals (e.g. cortisol) and suppresses inessential functions (e.g. digestion) in order to maintain internal stability. The effects of this are often expressed in terms of poor sleep and immune function, decreased cardiovascular health, and hormonal and metabolic dysfunction.[113] Overcrowding also contributes to the spread of communicable diseases that can further depress immune function (e.g. HIV and hepatitis).[114]

The CDCR's policy to exclude immunocompromised inmates from facilities in hyperendemic zones, and their decision to move vulnerable inmates from overcrowded institutions in endemic areas wrongly treats the surge in disease rates as an individual biomedical issue affecting raced bodies. As Krieger explains, the idea that certain racial groups are inherently more susceptible to disease imagines "race" as natural communities, and risks reinforcing stereotypes that portray racialised bodies as "naturally" defective, or biologically weak.[115] Biological determinism draws attention away from the carceral politics, environmental neglect, and structural inequalities that contribute to disease burden.

By positioning genetics as the primary cause of serious illness, the courts shifted attention away from the complex, layered, spatially dispersed, and trans-corporeal processes through which disease takes shape. In the case of Valley Fever, examining it through the lens of fungal agency and the dust politics of the American Plains suggests that its emergence may be an effect of a complex interplay between industrial agriculture, white supremacy, Indigenous dispossession, capitalist extractivism, environmental deregulation,

112 Gerald G Gaes, 'The Effects of Overcrowding in Prison' (1985) 6 Crime and Justice 95; Adrian M Ostfeld and others, *Stress, Crowding, and Blood Pressure in Prison* (Routledge 2023); 'The Wages of Prison Overcrowding: Harmful Psychological Consequences and Dysfunctional Correctional Reactions' (2006) 22 Washington University Journal of Law & Policy 265.

113 Peter C Konturek, T Brzozowski and SJ Konturek, 'Stress and the Gut: Pathophysiology, Clinical Consequences, Diagnostic Approach and Treatment Options' (2011) 62 Journal of Physiology and Pharmacology: An Official Journal of the Polish Physiological Society 591; Angel Fenol and others, 'Association of Stress, Salivary Cortisol Level, and Periodontitis among the Inmates of a Central Prison in Kerala' (2017) 14 Dental Research Journal 288.

114 Adeeba Kamarulzaman and others, 'Prevention of Transmission of HIV, Hepatitis B Virus, Hepatitis C Virus, and Tuberculosis in Prisoners' (2016) 388 The Lancet 1115; Ralf Jürgens, Manfred Nowak and Marcus Day, 'HIV and Incarceration: Prisons and Detention' (2011) 14 Journal of the International AIDS Society 26.

115 Nancy Krieger, 'The Science and Epidemiology of Racism and Health: Racial/Ethnic Categories, Biological Expressions of Racism, and the Embodiment of Inequality – an Ecosocial Perspective' in I Whitmarsh and DS Jones (eds), *What the Use of Race? Modern Governance and the Biology of Difference* (MIT Press 2010) 226.

and an individual-centred ethos that has continuously imagined "nature" as a commodity and resource for human-taking. These tracings cast doubt on the courts' insistence that infection is a matter of mere chance, reducible to the contingency of location and presumed genetic or medical predispositions. While infection may settle into the body as an act of chance, how it manifests, the intensity with which it proliferates, is an outcome of intersecting infrastructures, histories, and political economies that distribute vulnerability unevenly across human and more-than-human collectives.

Alarmingly, these fungal encounters are poised to become stronger. Researchers have found that climate change, by increasing the frequency of natural hazards like dust storms, wildfires, and drought, is likely to drive rates of Valley Fever even higher.[116] Dust storms in the American Southwest, for instance, are rising at a pace far above the global average.[117] At the same time, Cocci-endemic zones appear to be expanding, with climate-related dust conditions potentially creating new areas of risk.[118] In California alone, Valley Fever cases have increased fivefold over the past two decades, with more infections resulting in death.[119]

The CDCR's response and the courts' rulings reveal that state institutions approach Valley Fever through the conventional dualisms of western thought. Disease is framed either as a natural phenomenon, rooted in soil, climate, or genetics, and thus beyond legal or political responsibility, or as an institutional issue, limited to the actions and intentions of human agents within the prison system. This rigid separation between the natural and cultural overlooks how Valley Fever emerges from their entanglement. It is not purely biological or social, but a sociomaterial phenomenon shaped by the prison's deep entanglement with colonial, racial, and capitalist histories, histories that are made material through the land, climate, and microbial systems that surround and interact with carceral infrastructures and the bodies contained within them. Prisoners do not merely inhabit prisons; they are biologically transformed by them. Incarceration is not simply a juridical status, but a molecular condition.

The incarcerated body is where the enduring histories of colonial appropriation, racialised capitalism, industrial agriculture, climatological uncertainty,

116 Madelynn H Howard and others, 'Valley Fever under a Changing Climate in the United States' (2024) 193 Environment International 1; Kolivras and Comrie (n 28); Sarah J Coates and Lindy P Fox, 'Disseminated Coccidioidomycosis as a Harbinger of Climate Change' (2018) 4 JAAD Case Reports 424.

117 Aries C Keck, 'Dust Storms and Valley Fever in the American West' (*NASA News*, 2021) <https://www.nasa.gov/general/dust-storms-and-valley-fever-in-the-american-west/> accessed 6 October 2025.

118 McCotter and others (n 76) 1. Morgan E Gorris and others, 'Expansion of Coccidioidomycosis Endemic Regions in the United States in Response to Climate Change' (2019) 3 GeoHealth 308.

119 Howard and others (n 116).

changing soil conditions, and carceral ecologies converge. To say that we bear no responsibility for addressing this slow and steady accumulation of harms, shouldered by the most marginalised populations, and lured into being by the steadfast pursuit of human progress whatever the cost to (human and nonhuman) nature, is emblematic of why we find ourselves in the Anthropocene. By tracing the material emergence of Valley Fever, I hope I have provided an opening for new trajectories of thought about how, where, and whom we punish as a matter of environmental justice. Punishment in the Anthropocene requires big picture thinking that avoids falling into the trappings of immediacy and locality, to focus more crucially on the normative connections between the global and planetary flows of nature-culture.

Works Cited

Alaimo S, *Exposed* (University of Minnesota Press 2016).

Anderson D, 'Depression, Dust Bowl, Demography, and Drought: The Colonial State and Soil Conservation in East Africa during the 1930s' (1984) 83 African Affairs 321.

Aslani S and others, 'Epigenetic Alterations Underlying Autoimmune Diseases' (2016) 49 Autoimmunity 69.

Ben Sleeter, 'Late 20th Century Land Change in the Central Valley Ecoregion' (2008) 48 The California Geographer 27.

Berg MT and others, 'Losing Years Doing Time: Incarceration Exposure and Accelerated Biological Aging among African American Adults' (2021) 62 Journal of Health and Social Behavior 460.

Blaikie P and Brookfield H, 'Colonialism, Development and Degradation' in *Land Degradation and Society* (Routledge 1987).

Borchert J, 'The Dust Bowl in the 1970s' (1971) 61 Annals of the Association of American Geographers 1.

California S of, 'The Dust Bowl, California, and the Politics of Hard Times' (*California State Capitol Museum*) <https://capitolmuseum.ca.gov/exhibits/the-dust-bowl-california-and-the-politics-of-hard-times/> accessed 14 January 2025.

Castro-Lopez N and Hung C-Y, 'Immune Response to Coccidioidomycosis and the Development of a Vaccine' (2017) 5 Microorganisms 13.

Chief Moon-Riley K and others, 'The Biological Impacts of Indigenous Residential School Attendance on the next Generation' (2019) 7 SSM - Population Health 100343.

Chow NA and others, 'Factors Influencing Distribution of Coccidioides Immitis in Soil, Washington State, 2016' (2021) 6 mSphere e00598.

Coates SJ and Fox LP, 'Disseminated Coccidioidomycosis as a Harbinger of Climate Change' (2018) 4 JAAD Case Reports 424.

'Coccidioides Genomes' (*Broad Institute*, 3 June 2015) <https://www.broadinstitute.org/scientific-community/science/projects/fungal-genome-initiative/coccidioides-genomes> accessed 2 October 2025.

Coffman M, 'The Neurological Imprint of Incarceration and Its Effect on Recidivism' 37 Notre Dame Journal of Law, Ethics & Public Policy 2023.

Cole GT and others, 'Factors Regulating Morphogenesis in Coccidioides Immitis' in Hugo Vanden Bossche, Frank C Odds and David Kerridge (eds), *Dimorphic Fungi in Biology and Medicine* (Springer 1993).

Cox RA and Magee DM, 'Protective Immunity in Coccidioidomycosis: The Life Cycle and Biology of Coccidioides Immitis' (1998) 149 Research in Immunology 417.

Crum NF, 'Coccidioidomycosis: A Contemporary Review' (2022) 11 Infectious Diseases and Therapy 713.

Cutler DM, Miller G and Norton DM, 'Evidence on Early-Life Income and Late-Life Health from America's Dust Bowl Era' (2007) 104 Proceedings of the National Academy of Sciences 13244.

Dannenberg J, 'Valley Fever Declared a Public Health Emergency at Two California Prisons; Court Orders Prisoner Transfers' <https://www.prisonlegalnews.org/news/2013/jul/15/valley-fever-declared-a-public-health-emergency-at-two-california-prisons-court-orders-prisoner-transfers/>.

De La Cadena M and Blaser M (eds), *A World of Many Worlds* (Duke University Press 2018).

del Rocío Reyes-Montes M and others, 'The Habitat of Coccidioides Spp. and the Role of Animals as Reservoirs and Disseminators in Nature' (2016) 16 BMC Infectious Diseases 550.

Delaney D, *The Spatial, the Legal and the Pragmatics of World-Making* (Routledge 2010).

Egan T, *The Worst Hard Time* (Mariner Classics 2006).

Engelthaler DM, Chatters JC and Casadevall A, 'Was Coccidioides a Pre-Columbian Hitchhiker to Southcentral Washington?' (2023) 14 mBio <https://journals.asm.org/doi/10.1128/mbio.00232-23> accessed 10 July 2025.

Fanslow RA, 'The Migrant Experience | Articles and Essays | Voices from the Dust Bowl: The Charles L. Todd and Robert Sonkin Migrant Worker Collection, 1940-1941 | Digital Collections | Library of Congress' (*Library of Congress, Washington, D.C. 20540 USA*) <https://www.loc.gov/collections/todd-and-sonkin-migrant-workers-from-1940-to-1941/articles-and-essays/the-migrant-experience/> accessed 14 January 2025.

Fenol A and others, 'Association of Stress, Salivary Cortisol Level, and Periodontitis among the Inmates of a Central Prison in Kerala' (2017) 14 Dental Research Journal 288.

Ferry D, 'How the Government Put Tens of Thousands of People at Risk of a Deadly Disease' (*Mother Jones*, 2015) <https://www.motherjones.com/environment/2015/01/valley-fever-california-central-valley-prison/> accessed 27 June 2024.

Fite GC, 'Great Plains Farming: A Century of Change and Adjustment' (1977) 51 Agricultural History 244.

Fite GC, 'The Great Plains: A Colonial Area' (1961) 40 Current History 280.

Freedman M and others, 'Coccidioidomycosis Outbreaks, United States and Worldwide, 1940–2015' (2018) 24 Emerging Infectious Diseases 417.

Frost S, 'The Attentive Body: How the Indexicality of Epigenetic Processes Enriches Our Understanding of Embodied Subjectivity' (2020) 26 Body & Society 3.

Gaes GG, 'The Effects of Overcrowding in Prison' (1985) 6 Crime and Justice 95.

Gleick PH and Chalecki EL, 'The Impacts of Climatic Changes for Water Resources of the Colorado and Sacramento-San Joaquin River Basins' (1999) 35 JAWRA Journal of the American Water Resources Association 1429.

Gorris ME and others, 'Advocating for Coccidioidomycosis to Be a Reportable Disease Nationwide in the United States and Encouraging Disease Surveillance across North and South America' (2023) 9 Journal of Fungi 83.

Gorris ME and others, 'Expansion of Coccidioidomycosis Endemic Regions in the United States in Response to Climate Change' (2019) 3 GeoHealth 308.

Gregory JN, *American Exodus: The Dust Bowl Migration and Okie Culture in California* (Oxford University Press 1989).

Harden CP and Hyman GG, 'Agriculture and Soil Erosion' in Carol P Harden and Glenn G Hyman, *The Physical Geography of South America* (Oxford University Press 2007).

Harrison WR, 'Dangerous Dirt: Paleopathology of Valley Fever and the Biopolitics of Race' in *The Anthropology of Infectious Disease* (Routledge 1997).

Heijmans BT and others, 'Persistent Epigenetic Differences Associated with Prenatal Exposure to Famine in Humans' (2008) 105 Proceedings of the National Academy of Sciences 17046.

Hens K and Van Goidsenhoven L, 'Autism, Genetics and Epigenetics: Why the Lived Experience Matters in Research' (2017) 4 BioNews, December.

Hewagama A and Richardson B, 'The Genetics and Epigenetics of Autoimmune Diseases' (2009) 33 Journal of Autoimmunity 3.

Hirschmann JV, 'The Early History of Coccidioidomycosis: 1892–1945' (2007) 44 Clinical Infectious Diseases 1202.

Holleman H, *Dust Bowls of Empire: Imperialism, Environmental Politics, and the Injustice of 'Green' Capitalism* (Yale University Press 2018).

Howard MH and others, 'Valley Fever under a Changing Climate in the United States' (2024) 193 Environment International 1.

Hsu AP, 'The Known and Unknown "Knowns" of Human Susceptibility to Coccidioidomycosis' (2024) 10 Journal of Fungi.

Jenks JD and others, 'Race and Ethnicity: Risk Factors for Fungal Infections?' (2023) 19 PLOS Pathogens 1.

Jürgens R, Nowak M and Day M, 'HIV and Incarceration: Prisons and Detention' (2011) 14 Journal of the International AIDS Society 26.

Kamarulzaman A and others, 'Prevention of Transmission of HIV, Hepatitis B Virus, Hepatitis C Virus, and Tuberculosis in Prisoners' (2016) 388 The Lancet 1115.

Keck AC, 'Dust Storms and Valley Fever in the American West' (*NASA News*, 2021) <https://www.nasa.gov/general/dust-storms-and-valley-fever-in-the-american-west/> accessed 6 October 2025.

Kirkland TN and Fierer J, 'Coccidioidomycosis: A Reemerging Infectious Disease' (1996) 2 Emerging Infectious Diseases 192.

Kolivras KN and Comrie AC, 'Modeling Valley Fever (Coccidioidomycosis) Incidence on the Basis of Climate Conditions' (2003) 47 International Journal of Biometeorology 87.

Kollath DR, Miller KJ and Barker BM, 'The Mysterious Desert Dwellers: Coccidioides Immitis and Coccidioides Posadasii, Causative Fungal Agents of Coccidioidomycosis' (2019) 10 Virulence 222.

Konturek PC, Brzozowski T and Konturek SJ, 'Stress and the Gut: Pathophysiology, Clinical Consequences, Diagnostic Approach and Treatment Options' (2011) 62 Journal of Physiology and Pharmacology: An Official Journal of the Polish Physiological Society 591.

Krieger N, 'Methods for the Scientific Study of Discrimination and Health: An Ecosocial Approach' (2012) 102 American Journal of Public Health 936.

Krieger N, 'The Science and Epidemiology of Racism and Health: Racial/Ethnic Categories, Biological Expressions of Racism, and the Embodiment of Inequality – an Ecosocial Perspective' in I Whitmarsh and DS Jones (eds), *What the Use of Race? Modern Governance and the Biology of Difference* (MIT Press 2010).

Kulkarni S and others, 'Editorial: Epigenetics of Infectious Diseases' (2022) 13 Frontiers in Immunology.

Lacy GH and Swatek FE, 'Soil Ecology of Coccidioides Immitis at Amerindian Middens in California' (1974) 27 Applied Microbiology 379.

Long J and Siu HE, 'Refugees From Dust and Shrinking Land: Tracking the Dust Bowl Migrants' (National Bureau of Economic Research, March 2016) <https://www.nber.org/papers/w22108> accessed 14 January 2025.

Manzella AGH, *Migrating Fictions: Gender, Race, and Citizenship in U.S. Internal Displacements* (Ohio State University Press 2018).

Massoglia M, 'Incarceration as Exposure: The Prison, Infectious Disease, and Other Stress-Related Illnesses' (2008) 49 Journal of Health and Social Behavior 56.

Massoglia M and Pridemore WA, 'Incarceration and Health' (2015) 41 Annual Review of Sociology 291.

McCotter O and others, 'Coccidioidomycosis Among American Indians and Alaska Natives, 2001–2014' (2019) 6 Open Forum Infectious Diseases ofz052.

McCotter OZ and others, 'Update on the Epidemiology of Coccidioidomycosis in the United States' (2019) 57 Medical Mycology S30.

McLeman RA and others, 'What We Learned from the Dust Bowl: Lessons in Science, Policy, and Adaptation' (2014) 35 Population and Environment 417.

Mead HL and others, 'Coccidioidomycosis in Northern Arizona: An Investigation of the Host, Pathogen, and Environment Using a Disease Triangle Approach' (2022) 7 mSphere e00352.

Money NP, *Fungi: A Short Introduction* (OUP 2016).

Morris JM, 'When Corporations Rule the Llano Estacado: The Glorious Past and Uncertain Future of the Southern High Plains Family Farm' in Sherry Lynn Smith (ed), *The Future of the Southern Plains* (University of Oklahoma Press 2003).

Morrow W, 'Holocene Coccidioidomycosis: Valley Fever in Early Holocene Bison (Bison Antiquus)' (2006) 98 Mycologia 669.

Mulligan CJ, 'Systemic Racism Can Get under Our Skin and into Our Genes' (2021) 175 American Journal of Physical Anthropology 399.

Needham BL and others, 'Life Course Socioeconomic Status and DNA Methylation in Genes Related to Stress Reactivity and Inflammation: The Multi-Ethnic Study of Atherosclerosis' (2015) 10 Epigenetics 958.

Nguyen A, Knutson K and Djamba Y, 'Epidemiologic Summary of Valley Fever (Coccidioidomycosis) in California, 2020-2021' (California Department of Public Health 2021) Surveillance and Statistics Section <https://www.cdph.ca.gov/Programs/CID/DCDC/CDPH%20Document%20Library/CocciEpiSummary2020-2021.pdf> accessed 29 August 2025.

Nguyen T, 'The Dust Bowl Migration: Fear, Discrimination, Exclusion' (2018) 5 The Toro Historical Review.

Oldfield EC III and others, 'Prediction of Relapse After Treatment of Coccidioidomycosis' (1997) 25 Clinical Infectious Diseases 1205.

Ostfeld AM and others, *Stress, Crowding, and Blood Pressure in Prison* (Routledge 2023).

Park BJ and others, 'An Epidemic of Coccidioidomycosis in Arizona Associated with Climatic Changes, 1998–2001' (2005) 191 The Journal of Infectious Diseases 1981.

Pincetl SS, *Transforming California: A Political History of Land Use and Development* (John Hopkins University Press 2003).

Pisani DJ, *From the Family Farm to Agribusiness: The Irrigation Crusade in California and the West, 1850–1931* (University of California Press 2021).

Radosevich M and others, 'Characterizing the Soil Microbial Community Associated with the Fungal Pathogen Coccidioides Immitis' (2025) 11 Journal of Fungi <https://www.mdpi.com/2309-608X/11/4/309> accessed 6 October 2025.

Rios SM, 'Poverty, Prisons, Pollution and Valley Fever' in Michael Mascarenhas (ed), *Lessons in Environmental Justice: From Civil Rights to Black Lives Matter and Idle No More* (Sage Publications 2021), Chapter 12.

Robinette JW and Smith JA, 'Accelerated Molecular Aging in Socioeconomically Disadvantaged Neighborhoods: A Racial/Ethnic Comparison' (2025) 93 Health & Place 103446.

Salkin D and Said A, 'Reinfection with Coccidioidomycosis' (1993) 17 Clinical Infectious Diseases 1066.

Saubolle MA, McKellar PP and Sussland D, 'Epidemiologic, Clinical, and Diagnostic Aspects of Coccidioidomycosis' (2007) 45 Journal of Clinical Microbiology 26.

Saucier CJ and others, 'Overcoming Health Information Inequities: Valley Fever Information Repertoires Among Vulnerable Communities in California' (2024) 39 Health Communication 2793.

Sharpton TJ and others, 'Comparative Genomic Analyses of the Human Fungal Pathogens *Coccidioides* and Their Relatives' (2009) 19 Genome Research 1722.

Sheldrake M, *Entangled Life: How Fungi Make Our Worlds, Change Our Minds, and Shape Our Futures* (Vintage 2021).

Smith SL, *The Future of the Southern Plains* (University of Oklahoma Press 2003).

Southgate D, 'The Causes of Land Degradation along "Spontaneously" Expanding Agricultural Frontiers in the Third World' (1990) 66 Land Economics 93.

Strong JD and others, 'The Body in Isolation: The Physical Health Impacts of Incarceration in Solitary Confinement' (2020) 15 PLOS ONE e0238510.

Sullivan S, 'Inheriting Racist Disparities in Health: Epigenetics and the Transgenerational Effects of White Racism' (2013) 1 Critical Philosophy of Race 190.

Taylor JW and Barker BM, 'The Endozoan, Small-Mammal Reservoir Hypothesis and the Life Cycle of Coccidioides Species' (2019) 57 Medical Mycology S16.

Teirstein Z, 'Intensifying Atmospheric Rivers Are Leading to a Surge in Valley Fever Cases in California' (*Grist*, 12 February 2024) <https://grist.org/health/intensifying-atmospheric-rivers-are-leading-to-a-surge-in-valley-fever-cases-in-california/> accessed 29 August 2025.

Temple DH, 'A Possible Case of Coccidioidomycosis from the Los Muertos Site, Tempe, Arizona' (2006) 16 International Journal of Osteoarchaeology 316.

Thayer ZM and Kuzawa CW, 'Biological Memories of Past Environments: Epigenetic Pathways to Health Disparities' (2011) 6 Epigenetics 798.

'The History of Public Lands Grazing' (*Western Watersheds Project*) <https://westernwatersheds.org/the-history-of-public-lands-grazing/> accessed 11 July 2025.

'The Wages of Prison Overcrowding: Harmful Psychological Consequences and Dysfunctional Correctional Reactions' (2006) 22 Washington University Journal of Law & Policy 265.

Thompson J, 'Early Reclamation and Abandonment of the Central Sacramento-San Joaquin Delta' (2006) 6 Sacramento History Journal 41.

'Valley Fever: An Incurable Illness in the Dust' (*BBC News,* 16 July 2013) <https://www.bbc.com/news/magazine-23166839> accessed 2 October 2025.

Van Dyke MCC and others, 'The Rise of Coccidioides: Forces Against the Dust Devil Unleashed' (2019) 10 Frontiers in Immunology.

Voorhies M and others, '"Select and Resequence" Methods Enable a Genome-Wide Association Study of the Dimorphic Human Fungal Pathogen Coccidioides Posadasii' (2025) 17 Genome Biology and Evolution evaf135.

Wagner R and others, 'Coccidioides Undetected in Soils from Agricultural Land and Uncorrelated with Time or the Greater Soil Fungal Community on Undeveloped Land' (2023) 19 PLOS Pathogens e1011391.

Walton JS, 'Fit in Your Genes: An Introduction to Genes and Epigenetics for Forensic Practitioners' (2021) 23 The Journal of Forensic Practice, 189–200.

'Weekly Report of Population' (2025) SOMS-TPOP-1.

Wehrwein GS, 'A Land Policy as a Part of an Agricultural Program' (1925) 7 Journal of Farm Economics 289.

Werner SB and Pappagianis D, 'Coccidioidomycosis in Northern California—An Outbreak among Archeology Students near Red Bluff' (1973) 119 California Medicine 16.

West E, 'Trails and Footprints: The Past of the Future Southern Plains' in Sherry Lynn Smith (ed), *The Future of the Southern Plains* (University of Oklahoma Press 2003).

Whiston E and others, 'Comparative Transcriptomics of the Saprobic and Parasitic Growth Phases in Coccidioides Spp' (2012) 7 PLoS ONE e41034.

Worster D, *Dust Bowl: The Southern Plains in the 1930s* (Oxford University Press 2004).

Wrede D and others, 'Pulmonary Pathogen-Induced Epigenetic Modifications' (2023) 7 Epigenomes 13.

Yoo SD and others, 'Disseminated Coccidioidomycosis in Africa' (2020) 7 European Journal of Case Reports in Internal Medicine 001659.

Cases

Bates v Schwarzenegger [2020] Case No 19-17094 (9th Cir).

Beagle v Schwarzenegger [2014] Case No 1:14-cv-00430- LJO-SAB (ED Cal).

Brown v Plata (2011) 563 493 (US).

Chaney v Beard Case No 1:14-cv-00369-MJS (ED Cal).

Cunningham v Kramer [2016] 178 F Supp 3d 999 (ED Cal).

Franklin v Giurbino [2018] Case No 15-cv-04755-YGR (PR) (ND Cal).

Hines v Youseff [2019] 9th Cir 914 F.3d 1218.

Jackson v Brown [2015] Case No 1:13-cv-1055-LJO-SAB (ED Cal).

Nawabi v Cates [2015] Case No 1:13-cv-272-LJO-SAB (ED Cal).

Plata v Brown [2013] ND Cal No. 01-cv-01351.

Smith v Schwarzenegger [2015] Case No: 1:14-cv-00060-LJO-SAB.

4 (Capital) Punishment in the Chemosphere

For more than four centuries, the United States has used the death penalty to punish its most serious offenders, and for the last 40 years, it has carried it out using synthetic chemicals. Death penalty states have long promoted the idea that chemically induced executions are humane, and despite repeated public scenes of painful and violent executions,[1] this illusion of mercy continues to carry legal weight.[2] When executions go wrong, their legal defence often rests on a mechanistic view of Nature – where failures are portrayed as accidents, either natural anomalies or the product of simple human error.[3] In either case, the public is led to believe that failed executions are either too rare to merit concern or that their causes can be identified and prevented in future cases.

This chapter considers the normativity of Nature and its implications for punitive practice and experience from a slightly different, more controversial, perspective. While the previous chapter considered how the movements and activities of organisms, in active and vibrant habitats, shape and influence carceral ecologies and experiences of disease, here I examine the normativity of *non-living* Nature, the agency and norm-creating potential of chemicals. Specifically, I analyse the behaviour patterns of *synthetic* chemicals, which occupy an ontologically ambivalent position, simultaneously artificial and natural. The controversies of this approach arise from the fact that western philosophy has always ascribed special value and moral status to life, as opposed to nonlife. To then speak about nonlife as having agency, the capacity to act and affect, the ability to influence human normativity, is to shrink those boundaries between revered "life" and expendable "nonlife" even further. Nevertheless, exploring the failed execution as an act of chemical agency opens up possibilities for seeing its full range of political and cultural effects, and tracing how these localised "events" are enabled and constrained by global

1 Austin Sarat, *Gruesome Spectacles: Botched Executions and America's Death Penalty* (Stanford University Press 2016).
2 Eric Berger, 'Lethal Injection and the Problem of Constitutional Remedies' (2008) 27 Yale Law & Policy Review 259.
3 Sarat (n 1) 13–15.

DOI: 10.4324/9781003367567-5

politics and planetary flows and forces. The chemicals that state governments use to kill their condemned are not neutral tools in the commission of death; they are responsive, reactive, volatile entities. Any ethical discussion of capital punishment must therefore approach its use from an ecological perspective that understands chemical activity as relational and environmentally contingent.

In the first part of this chapter, I consider the controversies of the death penalty, the reasons why lethal injection is now the primary method of execution used by most death penalty states, on what basis its acceptability and legality are commonly challenged, and how penal institutions and legislators have responded to death penalty critics. Many of the existing justifications for lethal injection rely on knowledge that envisages chemicals as stable substances that have universal properties and calculable effects. Yet, there is much evidence to suggest that chemicals do not operate in accordance with the static rules devised by the (human) science of chemistry. Chemicals are recalcitrant creatures, promiscuous and temperamental.

In the second part of this chapter, I turn to the nature-culture ontology of chemicals, highlighting their entangled and pervasive presence in human and more-than-human life. I explore chemical recalcitrance by attending to how chemicals exercise agency, how they move with purpose, iterate across contexts, and form connective relations. Chemicals are not inert matter; they are lively, vibrant actors. I examine what this chemical vibrancy means for the practice of lethal injection. By the time you come to this chapter's close, I hope you will see that there is a life to chemicals that calls to be explored, a life that is legally interesting, and a life that discloses the death penalty as a toxic regime, upheld by exercises of colonial, corporatist, and classist power.

Death Penalty Aesthetics and Cruel and Unusual Punishment

In *Secrets of the Killing State*, Lain argues that lethal injection has become the dominant method of execution in the United States because of its ability to disguise the state's violence. In contrast to hanging, electrocution, or the gas chamber, which exposes witnesses to blood, burning flesh, and audible suffering, lethal injection conceals these visceral signs of killing. Its aesthetic of calm is not incidental but central to its appeal.[4] As Sarat observes, the lethal injection's internalised violence enables the state to mark a difference between its own "punitive violence" and the "criminal violence" it condemns, reassuring a public uneasy with overt brutality. The syringe, the IV line, the

4 Corinna Barrett Lain, *Secrets of the Killing State: The Untold Story of Lethal Injection* (New York University Press 2025) 4.

silent flow of chemicals all work to stage an execution that looks less like a killing and more like the administration of care.[5]

In most death penalty states, lethal injection proceeds, or has until very recently, through the sequential administration of three pharmacological agents. First, an anaesthetic, often an ultra-short or short-acting barbiturate such as sodium thiopental or pentobarbital, or more recently a benzodiazepine like midazolam; second, a paralytic that immobilises skeletal muscles, including the diaphragm which sustains breathing; and finally, an overdose of an antiarrhythmic that halts cardiac activity. The functional logic of the first and last drug is straightforward, the anaesthetic is meant to extinguish consciousness and sensation, while the antiarrhythmic induces death by halting heart function. But the paralytic occupies a more contested role.[6] Its purpose is less to kill than to condition the event of killing – silencing muscular convulsions, erasing signs of respiratory struggle, and rendering the body a still surface so that death can appear orderly.

Many argue that the paralytic's function is primarily aesthetic; it censors the body's struggle, erasing convulsions and silencing gasps, allowing the scene to be staged as measured and serene.[7] Yet, this chemical agent is not simply a neutral instrument. When the anaesthetic falters, the paralytic becomes a binding force, a "chemical straitjacket",[8] that immobilises muscles and locks the body into silence. In these instances, the inmate remains conscious to the effects of an antiarrhythmic that pulses in the form of burning veins, crushing suffocation, and a slow panic of being oxygen-deprived. The paralytic ensures that no signs of this inner anguish escape into the witness chamber to be seen by others.

For this reason, many death row inmates have challenged the use of the paralytic, claiming that the three-drug protocol risks transforming executions into a constitutionally impermissible form of cruel and unusual punishment.[9] Their objections find strong support in medical evidence. In the vast majority of 200 autopsies performed on executed inmates, physicians have found widespread evidence of pulmonary oedema, fluid-filled lungs consistent with death by drowning. These findings suggest that inmates may have experienced

5 Austin Sarat, *Lethal Injection and the False Promise of Humane Execution* (Stanford University Press 2022) 17.

6 Aaryn Urell, 'Lethal Injections Cause Suffocation and Severe Pain, Autopsies Show' (*Equal Justice Initiative*, 22 September 2020) <https://eji.org/news/lethal-injections-cause-suffocation-and-severe-pain-autopsies-show/> accessed 31 August 2025; Drew S Brazer, 'Lethal Paralytics and the Censorship of Suffering' (2023) 57 Columbia Journal of Law and Social Problems 1.

7 Brazer (n 6).

8 Ibid., 4.

9 *Glossip v Chandler* [2021] WD Okla CIV-14-0665-F.

extreme distress, difficulty breathing, and a sensation of drowning during the process of their execution.[10]

The political and legal history of lethal injection is troubling. Far from being grounded in medical science, it is a story of improvisation, speculation, and political expediency. First proposed as a tool of execution back in the nineteenth century, lethal injection was not formally adopted until nearly a century later.[11] The modern protocols were established in the 1970s by Oklahoma's Chief Medical Examiner, Dr. Chapman, a self-described "expert on dead bodies". By his own admission, the drug sequence he designed was largely untested and insufficiently researched for this purpose.[12] According to some reports, the use of the antiarrhythmic was originally recommended by a manufacturer of execution equipment who had no medical training, and who based his choice of chemicals on experiments that had been conducted on pigs.[13] Dr. Chapman's reasoning for including a paralytic was equally ad hoc: "why not?…You wanted to make sure the prisoner was dead at the end, so why not add a third drug?"[14] In his shrug of indifference, the paralytic entered into the pharmacological assemblage of state killing not as a medical necessity, but as a procedural afterthought.

Most death penalty states granted statutory approval to Chapman's improvised drug combination without conducting any independent research and dismissed its secondary effects as irrelevant as long as the inmate "ended up dead".[15] The same indifference has since shaped the drafting of new execution statutes and policies, many of which routinely invoke the requirement of a "fatal concentration" of chemicals without specifying the precise dosages or methods of calculation,[16] and in some cases without even specifying which lethal substances are to be used.[17] Here, the law does not so much prescribe a medical procedure as authorise a chemical event, leaving the procedural work of killing up to bureaucrats with no medical training and likely motivated by very different interests.

10 Joel B Zivot, Mark A Edgar and David A Lubarsky, 'Execution by Lethal Injection: Autopsy Findings of Pulmonary Edema' (medRxiv, 27 August 2022) <https://www.medrxiv.org/content/10.1101/2022.08.24.22279183v1> accessed 5 September 2024.

11 Sarat (n 5) 16.

12 Lain (n 4); Deborah W Denno, 'The Lethal Injection Quandary: How Medicine Dismantled the Death Penalty' (2007) 76 Fordham L. Rev. 49.

13 Andrew Fulkerson and Michael Suttmoeller, 'Current Issues Involving Lethal Injection' (2008) 21 Criminal Justice Studies 271, 273.

14 Lain (n 4) 30.

15 'So Long as They Die: Lethal Injections in the United States: I. Development of Lethal Injection Protocols' (*Human Rights Watch*, 2006) <https://www.hrw.org/reports/2006/us0406/3.htm> accessed 25 July 2025.

16 Ibid.

17 'IGA | 2024 Indiana Code' <https://iga.in.gov/laws/2024/ic/titles/35#35-38-6-1> accessed 27 July 2025 IC 35-38-6-1, Section 1(a)(1).

Since the lethal injection's inception, death penalty states have repeatedly revised their protocols, altering drug combinations and dosages in an ongoing process of trial and error, with little attention to the physiological consequences these new formulations may produce.[18] This experimentation occurs largely without medical oversight, as many professional associations prohibit medical personnel from participating in executions on ethical grounds.[19] Consequently, state protocols have evolved based primarily on drug availability, cost, and political expediency, rather than on wheher the procedure can deliver a "humane" death.[20]

This ad hoc approach to designing and redesigning the execution protocols has provoked a series of Eighth Amendment challenges from inmates, some of whom argue that they are being rendered unconscious using substances that have never been approved for anaesthetic use in human medicine.[21] Despite this checkered history, courts have declined to interrogate the pharmacological basis of lethal injection protocols, deferring instead to what they describe as "ongoing scientific controversies beyond their expertise".[22] Even when acknowledging that states have an obligation to disclose information to inmates about the drugs, manufacturers, and dosages that are to be used during their execution, their reasoning does not cite medical safety, but rather the need to ensure a process that remains "objectively" tolerable. Chemicals and protocols are recast as objects of political discourse, absorbed into the First Amendment's protection of free speech, press, assembly, and petition, where they circulate as matters of legal debate and political legitimacy.[23] In this process the body-in-pain is displaced by a disembodied legal rationality that privileges abstraction over sensation, procedure over experience. In so doing, the judiciary seems to have positioned itself outside the chemo-medical dimensions of execution, while simultaneously legitimising it. Instead, the burden is placed squarely on petitioners to not only show that the state's chosen compounds are incapable of delivering a humane death, but also to supply the court with alternative remedies,[24] effectively conscripting prisoners into the labour of designing their own execution.

Given its troubled lineage, it is unsurprising that many lethal injection executions do not go to plan. Sarat estimates that roughly three percent of all executions in the United States have been "botched" since the death penalty's

18 Deborah W Denno, 'Lethal Injection Chaos Post-Baze' (2013) 102 Georgetown Law Journal 1331.
19 Fulkerson and Suttmoeller (n 13) 274.
20 Denno (n 12) 65.
21 *Warner v Gross* (2015) 776 F3d 721 (10th Cir); *Bucklew v Precythe* [2019] 139 S Ct 1112.
22 *Baze v Rees* [2008] 553 US 35 Syllabus, para.1(d).
23 *Wood v Ryan* [2014] 759 F 3d 1076 (9th Cir).
24 *Glossip v Gross* [2015] 135 S Ct 2726.

inception.[25] With the adoption of lethal injection that figure has more than doubled.[26] Some researchers suggest that in more recent cases, the failure rate may be as high as 37 percent.[27] For its critics, these flawed executions offer a fleeting window into the hidden suffering that occurs during the process, a suffering normally obscured from view.[28] As Borg and Radelet observe, one might assume that a nation capable of sending humans to the moon with exact precision would also be able to "shoot people into the hereafter" with similar technical certainty.[29] Viewed through this lens, the inconsistencies of lethal injection emerge not merely as moral failings, but as a failure of procedural "science" itself.

From a scientific standpoint, the imprecision of the lethal injection can be traced in part to the fact that many of the drugs being employed were never engineered for the purpose of ending human life. Consequently, empirical data on their efficacy in this context is minimal. In existing studies, toxicity is treated as a side effect of their misuse or abuse, rendering any conclusions about their capacity to kill largely speculative. Within the framework of constitutional challenges, courts have consistently explained the state's experiments with these chemicals as unproblematic.[30] In their view, the law allows for procedural innovation in administering capital punishment as long as the state's experimentation does not clearly violate constitutional protections. Given the absence of *in vivo* data, petitioners must thus wait for an execution to go wrong before they can challenge the constitutionality of the state's drug combination. The courts have further affirmed that executions always carry with them the potential to be painful and complicated because human actors remain fallible; "there is always the possibility of human error or unfortunate misadventure".[31] There is a long legal history of framing failed executions as errors, linked to either procedural blunders or impure or improperly sourced chemicals – failures traced not to chemical agency, but to the network of human handlers, distributors, manufacturers, and administrators.[32] Through

25 Sarat (n 1).

26 Jack Kevorkian, 'Medicine, Ethics, and Execution by Lethal Injection' (1985) 4 Medicine and Law 307.

27 'As Lethal Injection Turns Forty, States Botch a Record Number of Executions' (Death Penalty Information Center, 2022) <https://deathpenaltyinfo.org/news/as-lethal-injection-turns-forty-states-botch-a-record-number-of-executions> accessed 8 August 2024.

28 Lain (n 4) 3.

29 Marion J Borg and Michael L Radelet, 'On Botched Executions' in Peter Hodgkinson and William A Schabas (eds), Capital Punishment: Strategies for Abolition (Cambridge University Press 2004) 143.

30 *Re Ohio Execution Protocol Litigation* [2014] 994 F Supp 2d 906 (SD Ohio) 913.

31 Ibid.

32 Teri Schultz, 'Europe Fights the Death Penalty — with Drugs' (*The World from PRX*, 2 August 2016) <https://theworld.org/stories/2016/08/02/europe-fights-death-penalty-drugs> accessed 9 May 2025.

this framing, chemical misbehaviour becomes a system-level instability, a predictable glitch in the interface between human imperfection and the mechanised protocols for ending life, all of which leave us with the false sense that these failures are correctable.

Living in a Chemosphere

The chemicals used by the state to carry out the death penalty circulate within wider ecological networks, entangling human and nonhuman actors alike. Consequently, thinking about what these chemicals can do in "our" world requires an understanding of how they connect, shape, and are reconstituted by "their" surroundings. Chemicals are not passive substances manipulated by human will; they are active participants in proliferating networks of interaction, not only connecting human and nonhuman worlds with one another but also constituting and assembling the very entities that comprise them.

Humans live in a chemosphere, a chemically-mediated world that connects us to the environment in the form of elemental and chemical relations.[33] Humans are, as Dennis writes, "chemical species embedded in chemical ecologies".[34] The chemosphere is vibrant and relational, capable of communicating across itself because, at a molecular level, everything that is part of it (humans included) is composed of the same bits of matter, the same "elements". Carbon, hydrogen, nitrogen, and oxygen – the so-called "building blocks" of life – facilitate interaction between living things, achieved through the absorption and release of chemicals and electrical signals. But even nature's non-living beings, its winds, sunlight, waters, mountains, volcanoes, and soils, interact with one another and with the living world in the form of chemical or elemental interplays.[35]

Chemical relationality is a precondition for human life. From the time we are zygotes, we exist in chemically saturated environments, mediated through a complex blend of hormones, enzymes, proteins, and lipids which regulate every aspect of our early existence and growth. Once we are born, we live by "taking in" our world through sensory organs that use a combination of chemical and electrical signals to give form and meaning to the environment

33 Nicholas Shapiro, 'Attuning to the Chemosphere: Domestic Formaldehyde, Bodily Reasoning, and the Chemical Sublime' (2015) 30 Cultural Anthropology 368.

34 Fay Dennis, 'Chemical Species: The Art and Politics of Living with(out) Drugs after Addiction' (2023) 18 BioSocieties 545, 546.

35 Hirokazu Ueda, Yukio Kikuta and Kazuhiko Matsuda, 'Plant Communication: Mediated by Individual or Blended VOCs?' (2012) 7 Plant Signaling & Behavior 222; Julie F Hill and Valerie Olson, 'The Chemical Kinship of Stony Entities' <http://juliefhill.co.uk> accessed 25 July 2025; Michelle Murphy, 'Alterlife and Decolonial Relations' (2017) 32 Cultural Anthropology 494; Christer Brönmark and Lars-Anders Hansson, 'Chemical Communication in Aquatic Systems: An Introduction' (2000) 88 Oikos 103.

we physically encounter. Life in our world is shaped by the presence of not only naturally occurring chemicals, generated through biological and geological processes, but also synthetic or "anthropogenic chemicals",[36] produced by industries in pursuit of human ends. These chemical ecologies induce the "everyday experience of rootedness and belonging in our surroundings…Elements and anthropogenic molecules shape human bodies and human action as much as human affects and imaginaries".[37]

The extent to which we are embedded in, conditioned by, and generated through chemical worlds, natural and synthetic, reveals a kind of "alterlife", that is provisional, relational, and co-produced by intra-actions between chemicals, technologies, and social practice.[38] Chemical exposure is an inescapable quality of contemporary human life. We cannot eat, breathe, sleep, or work without coming up against chemicals of some form, both natural and synthetic. But these chemical exposures are unevenly distributed, often entangled with questions of gender, class, and race. Exposures can manifest in bodies as "chemically altered metabolisms, [differential] capacities to digest human-made substances, or bodily phenotypes that develop in responsiveness to both chosen and unchosen chemicals and pharmaceuticals".[39] From the toxic compounds produced by fungi and which can contaminate the crops and plants that we feast on,[40] to the chemicals that line our building materials and are unknowingly inhaled to become part of our visceral makeup as precursors of disease,[41] to the volatile organic compounds and chemical pheromones that plants secrete to encourage the pollination of blooms that have become cultural metaphors,[42] chemicals infuse our environments, invade our bodies, shape our moods, drive our politics, and condition our cultures. These chemical exposures and permeations can "bind" us as social communities, occupying a particular temporal and spatial moment,[43] and can reveal important insights about the world(s) we inhabit, the kinds of values and ethical concerns that preoccupy us, and the kinds of political norms and legal rules

36 Dimitris Papadopoulos, 'Chemicals, Ecology, and Reparative Justice' in Dimitris Papadopoulos, Maria Puig de la Bellacasa and Natasha Myers (eds), *Reactivating Elements: Chemistry, Ecology, Practice* (Duke University Press 2021). 34–69.

37 Ibid., 37, 43.

38 Michelle Murphy, 'Current Book in Progress' (13 November 2007) <https://michellemurphy.net/technoscience-meets-biopolitics/> accessed 30 July 2025.

39 Murphy, 'Alterlife and Decolonial Relations' (n 35) 497–8.

40 Mohamed E Zain, 'Impact of Mycotoxins on Humans and Animals' (2011) 15 Journal of Saudi Chemical Society 129.

41 Shapiro (n 33).

42 Florian P Schiestl, 'The Evolution of Floral Scent and Insect Chemical Communication' (2010) 13 Ecology Letters 643.

43 Max Liboiron, Manuel Tironi and Nerea Calvillo, 'Toxic Politics: Acting in a Permanently Polluted World' (2018) 48 Social Studies of Science 331, 331; Papadopoulos (n 1); Stacy Alaimo, Exposed (University of Minnesota Press 2016).

that we have in place.[44] Our body chemistry is the site where our material and cultural worlds collide. We live "within and are made up of ever-changing chemical flows",[45] and to such measure that it becomes difficult to distinguish human as a "being" that is separate from its chemical processes of "becoming", its chemical kinships.

It is not only human life, but also human nonlife, that is chemically mediated. Human biological death materialises through profound alterations to body chemistry, shaped by the chemical processes of deoxygenation, acidosis, and putrefaction. This has led some to argue that a decaying corpse, the epitome of human nonlife, is in fact an ecology "teeming *with* life" if we drill down into its chemical processes.[46] Humans live with and through the chemosphere; our chemical composition and our chemical exposures have implications not only for our politics, but also for the "corporeal substance" of our bodies,[47] and for human biological life across temporal scales.[48] So pervasive are the effects of chemicals that we manufacture and encounter that they are capable of intervening in the life opportunities and experiences of bodies yet-to-come.[49] The chemical processes that bodies undergo, the chemical relationships that they form, and the chemical structures they embody can give us an understanding of the kind of (biocultural) world in which they live.

Chemicals as Sociomaterial Assemblages

All of this is not to say that chemicals are "natural" phenomena. Human societies have long tried to make sense of their place within this chemicalised world by finding ways of ordering it, controlling it, and deploying it to their advantage. Chemistry, the scientific study of these reagents that shape our lives, suggests that chemicals are composed of base elements, sometimes on their own, and other times in combination with other elements that have

44 A Balayannis and E Garnett, 'Chemical Kinship: Interdisciplinary Experiments with Pollution' (2020) 6 Catalyst: Feminism, Theory, Technoscience 1; Vanessa Agard-Jones, 'Bodies in the System' (2013) 17 Small Axe 182; Emma Cardwell, 'Moral Economies of Life and Death: Agricultural Improvement, Imperialism, and Chemical Kinships with Reactive Nitrogen' (2023) 9 Catalyst: Feminism, Theory, Technoscience <https://catalystjournal.org/index.php/catalyst/article/view/38415> accessed 24 September 2024.

45 Dennis (n 34) 545.

46 Mo Costandi, 'Life after Death: The Science of Human Decomposition' *The Guardian* (5 May 2015) <https://www.theguardian.com/science/neurophilosophy/2015/may/05/life-after-death> accessed 22 July 2025.

47 Stacy Alaimo, *Bodily Natures: Science, Environment, and the Material Self* (Indiana University Press 2010).

48 Julia Kuznetski (Née Tofantšuk) and Stacy Alaimo, 'Transcorporeality: An Interview with Stacy Alaimo' (2020) 11 Ecozon@: European Journal of Literature, Culture and Environment 137.

49 Ibid.; Stacy Alaimo, *Exposed* (University of Minnesota Press 2016); Murphy, 'Current Book in Progress' (n 38).

been painstakingly recorded in what is perhaps the most enduring artefact of modern chemistry, Mendeleev's Periodic Table. Displaying all the different elements "discovered" by modern science, arranged in order of their atomic weight and grouped together by shared chemical characteristics and properties, the periodic table is not just a scientific tool but also a cultural symbol of order and structure in a world that often presents as random and chaotic.[50]

Yet, the periodic table's neat categories mask complexity. Its structure has sparked longstanding debate over whether classification should rest on the observable properties or atomic structure of elements.[51] We know, for instance, that carbon atoms can manifest in many different material forms – as charcoal, plastics, diamonds, and graphite depending on temperature, pressure, or the presence of a catalyst. These environmental conditions can shape not only carbon's form and behaviour, but also its social uses. The physical properties, appearance, and social uses of carbon fluctuate with its habitat, and whether carbon presents as coal, plastic, or diamond has implications for human norms and law.[52]

That is not to say that carbon's atomic structure offers a more stable foundation for understanding the element. Modern chemistry, established on Lavoisier's view of elements as "elementary" entities incapable of being chemically decomposed any further,[53] has been dealt quite a blow by developments in nuclear physics, which show that an element's atomic structure and weight can be altered without affect to its chemical properties, and that even basic elements are capable of becoming something new as a result of radioactive decay. Accordingly, even elements, the basic building blocks of chemicals, are not immutable, but dynamic participants in chemical life – unstable, relational, and always in the process of becoming in conjunction with their surrounding environment.

Otherwise abstract entities, chemicals have been given presence and form through scientific experiments and arrangements often deployed as objective truths.[54] As Helmreich explains, "chemical elements become thinkable through theory; they are not so much discovered as *envisaged.* That envisaging, coupled with experiment, can even be mobilised to create – and not just predict – new elements: representing, intervening, making".[55] What elements *become* is not simply about their intrinsic properties, or mechanical pro-

50 Primo Levi, *The Periodic Table* (Penguin 1986).

51 Jonathan Simon and Bernadette Bensaude-Vincent, *Chemistry: The Impure Science (Second Edition)* (World Scientific Publishing Company 2012) 155–8.

52 Ben Fine, 'Coal, Diamonds and Oil: Toward a Conparative Theory of Mining? *' (1994) 6 Review of Political Economy 279.

53 Antonine Lavoisier, *Elements of Chemistry: In a New Systematic Order, Containing All the Modern Discoveries* (Robert Kerr tr, Fifth Edinburgh Edition, Evert Duyckinck 1806).

54 Simon and Bensaude-Vincent (n 51) 160.

55 Stefan Helmreich, 'Elementary Forms of Elementary Forms: Old, New, and Wavy' in Dimitris Papadopoulos, Maria Puig de la Bellacasa and Natasha Myers (eds), *Reactivating Elements: Chemistry, Ecology, Practice* (Duke University Press 2021) 73.

cesses, but how those properties are "brought out", signified, and/or brought to bear on the world through the injection of other (human and nonhuman) forces, technologies, and epistemologies[56] – the geophysical pressures and temperatures that convert carbon atoms into diamonds, or the introduction of cracking technology to transform the same atoms into polymers, and/or the knowledge systems which document these practices, making them accessible and functional. How humans behave around carbon, what laws they establish, even what feelings are invoked and the stories they inspire,[57] will vary based on whether humans encounter carbon as a synthetic polymer, or a mineralised stone, or a radioactive isotope. Carbon is able to elicit different actions, feelings, behaviours, and politics based on the assemblages that it forms, but also by the cultural constructs through which it materialises. Nevertheless, as Papadopoulos explains, this is also not an element's whole story.

We can never know, with any certainty, what an element is capable of. . To a certain extent, we know what some elements can do in *certain ecologies*. The ecological and epistemological conditions through which an element emerges and acts, constrain and enable what it is able to do and become. We might go as far as to say that elements possess a kind of vitality that is brought out through their intra-action with the environment writ large. Chemicals, as elemental entities, may have capacities that remain hidden until the right conditions for their emergence materialise. In this sense, as Barad and Bennett's understanding of matter suggests, chemical agency is not so much possessed as *enacted* by its relationality with other forces, technologies, and entities in the unfolding of phenomena.[58]

Given that every aspect of human life and death is chemically mediated, the claim that chemical patterns of behaviour, "chemo-norms", are capable of enabling and constraining human normativity seems somewhat obvious. Human agency is indelibly linked with chemical activity. Yet, we rarely conceptualise chemicals as possessing "self-directed constitutive normativity".[59] Instead, our picture of chemicals is that they are inert substances, whose primary function is to serve human ends. By adopting a teleological understanding of chemicals, recognising their movements as having a direction that may not always align with human pursuits and interests, we give ourselves the opportunity to *think about them* differently, and to use them to think about *ourselves* differently. Schelling explains this beautifully:

56 Papadopoulos (n 36) 42–3.

57 HD Crider, 'The Story of the Diamond' (1924) 9 The American Midland Naturalist 176.

58 Karen Barad, *Meeting the Universe Halfway: Quantum Physics and the Entanglement of Matter and Meaning* (Duke University Press 2007) 97–132; Jane Bennett, *Vibrant Matter: A Political Ecology of Things* (Duke University Press 2010) 20–51.

59 Davies, Ecolaw, 53.

> So long as I myself am *identical* with Nature, I understand what a living nature is as well as I understand my own life; I apprehend how this universal life of Nature reveals itself in manifold forms, in progressive developments, in gradual approximations to freedom. As soon, however, as I separate myself, and with me everything ideal from Nature, nothing remains to me but a dead object, and I cease to comprehend how a life outside me can be possible.[60]

Working from this view of Nature-human connectedness, let us now turn to the chemical life of barbiturates, sedative anaesthetics that have been the primary, and in some instances the sole, chemicals used to execute inmates, in all 27 death penalty states. Let us explore how a nature-culture view of chemicals can prompt us to think about the life and activity of barbiturates differently.

Barbiturate Alterlife

Barbiturates are synthetic chemicals, originally derived from the raw materials of mineral deposits combined with proteins found in the liver of animals. Accordingly, they possess a strange ontology as, at once, fabricated and organic, true materialisations of nature-culture. While chemically formulated in 1881 by two German scientists, the first pharmacologically active barbiturate was synthesised in 1902 and soon marketed by the German company Farben Bayer, under the trade name Veronal.[61] Its commercialisation revolutionised pharmacological approaches to neuro-psychological disorders of the time and facilitated the treatment of psychoses, sleep disorders, and epileptic seizures. Veronal was also revered for its anaesthetic properties and, soon after its introduction to commercial markets, was readily used as a sedative for minor surgical procedures.[62]

Barbiturates are capricious creatures. In human bodies, their molecules are lured to receptor-sites in the central nervous system by long-range electrostatic forces. They approach these protein complexes in the hopes of discovering a temporary companion for a fleeting assemblage. As agonists, barbiturates do not simply "activate" receptors; they intervene in the body's

60 Friedrich Wilhelm Joseph von Schelling and Keith R Peterson, *First Outline of a System of the Philosophy of Nature* (State University of New York Press 2004) xx.

61 Francisco López-Muñoz, Ronaldo Ucha-Udabe and Cecilio Alamo, 'The History of Barbiturates a Century after Their Clinical Introduction' (2005) 1 Neuropsychiatric Disease and Treatment 329, 332.

62 Ibid., 329.

affective and metabolic rhythms, modulating patterns of excitation and rest.[63] Within these molecular assemblages, agency is diffuse, shared between molecules, receptors, and the human organism that hosts them. At higher concentrations, however, this balance of agency shifts and barbiturates go from being gentle modulators to commanding dictators. In this state, barbiturate molecules reconfigure the body's internal economies of mood and energy, instituting new thresholds of normality and dependence, compelling higher and higher doses to maintain equilibrium.[64] In this state, the chemical processes they provoke can be habit-forming and lethal to their human hosts.[65]

The transformation of barbiturates from experimental laboratory curiosities to marketable commodities hinges on a small molecular alteration – the replacement of a single carbon atom at position five, with a hydrogen-carbon compound; an intervention that was originally celebrated as the discovery of its parent compound's "true" hypnotic character[66] and stealthily protected through the application of a legal patent. These practices transformed what was an intervention into an invention. Ontologically abstract and otherwise insensible, the chemical flows of barbituric acid were crystallised in a form that gave meaning, purpose, and value to its carbon-5 configuration. In the true fashion of European imperialism, the legal claim over Veronal relied on the doctrine of discovery and the post-Enlightenment view that any contribution of human labour – physical, intellectual, monetary – is capable of converting Nature into property, granting its proprietors private ownership rights over its processes of becoming. In another twist, Veronal was later marketed as "Barbital" in the United States. Originally synthesised and patented in Germany, a world-renowned leader in pharmaceutical manufacturing,[67] the legal rights to this chemical were transferred to the Americans as a "kind of war booty" after the First World War.[68] Barbital was thus enacted through an entanglement between the sedative-hypnotic chemo-norms of barbituric acid, commodified through the social norms of laboratory science and the pharmaceutical industry, the political norms of war, and the legal norms of patents and commercial rights.

63 Michael J Neal, *Medical Pharmacology at a Glance* (Proquest Ebook Central, John Wiley & Sons 2015) 25.

64 Carl D Chambers, Leon Brill and James A Inciardi, 'Barbiturate Use, Misuse and Abuse' (1972) 2 Journal of Drug Issues 15, 16.

65 MM Glatt, 'The Abuse of Barbiturates in the United Kingdom' [1962] UNODC (United Nations Office on Drugs and Crime) <//www.unodc.org/unodc/en/data-and-analysis/bulletin/bulletin_1962-01-01_2_page004.html> accessed 29 July 2025.

66 López-Muñoz, Ucha-Udabe and Alamo (n 61) 332.

67 Alfred S Burdick, 'The Manufacture of Synthetic Medicinal Chemicals in America*' (1922) 11 The Journal of the American Pharmaceutical Association (1912) 98.

68 López-Muñoz, Ucha-Udabe and Alamo (n 61) 332.

In its heyday, between 1939 and 1960, the American sale of Barbital rose to more than 2,000 tonnes. As one author describes the scene, "[f]or reasons of frustration, desperation, or simply foolishness, the American public was gulping barbiturates" in higher and higher quantities, and much of this consumption was not medically prescribed. Millions of these capsulised chemicals flowed across American borders illegally through Mexico,[69] sustaining a population that was quickly becoming hooked on its effects. The fatality and dependency rates associated with barbiturate intoxication are the reasons why its clinical use has steadily declined over the decades, and medical professionals have lobbied governments to enact legislation reclassifying this chemical as a "narcotic" so that its manufacture and distribution can be better controlled.[70]

Barbital activity is environmentally contingent. As a polymorphic compound, it is capable of crystallising in different patterns, and the shape that it takes can affect its solubility, thermodynamic stability, and absorption rates. All of these properties can influence Barbital's clinical efficacy and safety. What this also means is that the environmental conditions under which Barbital is produced, stored, and administered can influence how it behaves once administered to humans.[71] Manufactured as salts, Barbital must be converted to a solution before its anaesthetic properties become accessible. In combination with a diluent, Barbital can be injected intravenously, where its sedative-hypnotic effects are immediate, and its duration of action prolonged. But in this change of state, Barbital also becomes more unstable, vulnerable to chemical and microbial intra-action, sensitive to changes in light and temperature, and capable of having its chemical properties altered by exposure to air. Any of these entanglements may cause Barbital to behave differently – decompose, degrade, form precipitates – all of which make it difficult to predict its future behaviour.[72] Barbital is most potent as an anaesthetic in its most unstable chemical form.

By tinkering with the atomic structure of Barbital, replacing the atoms of one element with atoms of another, chemists in laboratories across the globe have tried to improve the potency and active duration of this chemical. One result of this dabbling was the synthesis of Pentothal, the trade name for sodium thiopental, an ultra-short acting barbiturate that was used for lethal

69 Dimitri A Cozanitis, 'One Hundred Years of Barbiturates and Their Saint' (2004) 97 Journal of the Royal Society of Medicine 594, 596.

70 Ibid., 596–7.

71 Neslihan Zencirci and others, 'Crystal Polymorphs of Barbital: News about a Classic Polymorphic System' (2014) 11 Molecular Pharmaceutics 338.

72 Sydney M Priest and Timothy P Geisbuhler, 'Injectable Sodium Pentobarbital: Stability at Room Temperature' (2015) 76 Journal of Pharmacological and Toxicological Methods 38; William P Eckel, Benjamin Ross and Robert K Isensee, 'Pentobarbital Found in Ground Water' (1993) 31 Groundwater 801.

injections until 2010. While the discovery of Pentothal gained international acclaim from the scientific world, the world that unfolds in strictly controlled laboratories and through regimented experimentation in the world at large, where environmental conditions fluctuate, the risks associated with its use seemed to multiply.

In one study on military casualties of Pearl Harbor, researchers determined that Pentothal behaved differently in patients who had suffered extreme physical and psychiatric trauma.[73] According to one surgical doctor who worked at Pearl Harbor, these nuances of Pentothal behaviour were likely to go unnoticed by medical professionals involved in war surgery because they had little to no experience in "the art of" anaesthetics.[74] Under violent wartime conditions, Pentothal undertook new pathways of action, revealing previously concealed chemical capacities and generating new norms of behaviour that may have started at the molecular level, but eventually became global in effect. For decades after Pearl Harbor, Pentothal was mythologised as an object of fear across the medical profession internationally, and many stories were told about how the surgical use of this chemical agent may have contributed to killing more military men than the Japanese attack itself.[75] The "anaesthetic" events of Pearl Harbor exposed a need for more research and specialised training in the administration of anaesthetics and eventually led to the institutionalisation of modern Anaesthesiology as a distinctive field of study.[76]

Interestingly, much later in 1995, research conducted by Bennetts appeared to suggest that this almost folkloric image of Pentothal that had emerged after Pearl Harbor could partly be attributed to wartime censorship and the United States military's overall imprecise wartime record-keeping. For Bennetts, this may have contributed to overestimating the chemical's connection to the surgical fatality rate[77] and may have helped to promote the "scare-stories" that emerged as a result. But these scare-stories were potent enough to cause medical professionals, particularly in the United States, to reduce their overall use of Pentothal as a surgical anaesthetic, even by the very same physicians who had originally introduced it into clinical practice as an effective alternative to other medicines.[78]

The war-torn bodies of Pearl Harbor thus gave rise to new chemosocial alliances such that "even as we scaled inward to [the] body's most mundane functions, by proxy we were also scaling outward to talk about" developments

73 FJ Halford, 'A Critique of Intravenous Anesthesia in War Surgery' (1943) 4 Anesthesiology 67.

74 Ibid., 67–8.

75 John A Crowhurst, 'The Legacy of the Anaesthesia Events at Pearl Harbor, 7th December 1941.' (2016) 24 Journal of Military and Veteran's Health 52.

76 Ibid.

77 FE Bennetts, 'Thiopentone Anaesthesia at Pearl Harbour' (1995) 75 British Journal of Anaesthesia 366, 366.

78 Crowhurst (n 75) 53.

in modern medicine, the distribution of wartime medical technologies, the circulation of cultural narratives, and the politics of eastern expansionism coming to a head with western imperialism.[79] Zooming in on Pentothal allowed us to discover the extent to which bodies move and exist within multiscalar "systems" of power, bringing into sharper relief how "small places" (like makeshift surgical wards in Pearl Harbor), and "marginal people" (like wartime surgeons), can become "central to social analyses".[80] Pentothal took on global cultural significance by shaping political and medical discourse.

But the anaesthetic events of Pearl Harbor also deserve attention for the fact that they expose barbiturate activity as environmentally contingent. Pearl Harbor was not a simple case of medical malpractice. Its anaesthetic events cannot be explained away as simple matters of learning about how barbiturates behave when administered to patients suffering from war trauma. These are not matters of how humans have fallen short but matters that expose chemical agency and relationality. Injectable Pentothal is unpredictable. It is capable of forming quick relations with its surroundings and altering its patterns of "normal" behaviour in response. Couple this with the fact that what we often term "trauma" is itself marked by multiplicities in form and intensity, materialised through a range of complex and dynamic physiological and psychological processes. Injected into such dynamic conditions, it is impossible to predict how Pentothal is likely to react. Researchers have indicated that many of the biochemical effects of bodily trauma *in vivo* are dramatically different from what can be modelled in experimental settings that simulate such events. Attempts to replicate the conditions of Nature in a laboratory not only challenge the very epistemic foundations of Nature itself, but also cannot be done with any real accuracy given the dynamicity of Nature and the heterogeneity of bodies themselves.[81]

In 2010, after a series of legal challenges regarding its effectiveness and a European ban on its export to countries that use it for the death penalty,[82] Pentothal was replaced by Pentobarbital as the primary chemical used in lethal injections. Long employed as a euthanising agent for animals, a single dose of Pentobarbital could both anaesthetise inmates and stop cardiac function. As a result, many correctional institutions revised their lethal injection procedures, replacing the three-drug combination with a single fatal dose of Pentobarbital.

79 Agard-Jones (n 44) 183.

80 Ibid.

81 Jordi L Tremoleda and others, 'Modeling Acute Traumatic Hemorrhagic Shock Injury: Challenges and Guidelines for Preclinical Studies' (2017) 48 Shock 610; Carl J Hauser, 'Preclinical Models of Traumatic, Hemorrhagic Shock' (2005) 24 Shock 24.

82 Chris McGreal, 'Lethal Injection Drug Production Ends in the US' *The Guardian* (23 January 2011) <https://www.theguardian.com/world/2011/jan/23/lethal-injection-sodium-thiopental-hospira> accessed 16 October 2025.

While debates rage on about its legality and ethics in the realm of capital punishment,[83] Pentobarbital's environmental afterlife is a quieter, more insidious consequence that often escapes public attention. Pentobarbital is not a fleeting substance; its effects linger long after an execution ends. When administered in lethal doses to animals and humans, its relatively long half-life means that it is never fully metabolised by the body before the onset of death. At these levels, the chemical can maintain an undecayed presence in tissues and organs several years after host decomposition.[84] Over time, traces of this drug have been detected in soil and groundwater, especially near landfills that receive medical waste or areas where animals are chemically euthanised. From there, it becomes part of the environment's hidden flow, riding in leachate and runoff, entering ecosystems that were never its target. In waterways, Pentobarbital poses a threat to aquatic life and microorganisms, and has even been found in drinking water supplies.[85] Wildlife and domestic animals that scavenge euthanised carcasses or are fed rendered products may inadvertently ingest the drug, leading to secondary poisoning that can be fatal.[86] The higher the doses of Pentobarbital used, the greater its environmental residue.

In soil, the degradation of Pentobarbital is largely achieved through the activity of *Rhodococcus erythropolis* (*R. erythropolis*), a species of bacteria naturally found in contaminated environments. Hardy creatures that can survive and adapt to hostile habitats by changing their shape and binding their cells together to form superstructures,[87] *R. erythropolis* produce a variety of enzymes capable of breaking down many different fat-loving and

83 Erik Ortiz and Abigail Brooks, 'In Texas, New Details about Its Execution Drug Underscore a Closely Guarded Secret' (*NBC News*, 14 October 2025) <https://www.nbcnews.com/news/us-news/texas-new-details-execution-drug-underscore-closely-guarded-secret-rcna236168> accessed 16 October 2025; Susie Neilson, 'Lethal Injection Drugs' Efficacy And Availability For Federal Executions' *NPR* (26 July 2019) <https://www.npr.org/2019/07/26/745722219/lethal-injection-drugs-efficacy-and-availability-for-federal-executions> accessed 16 October 2025; 'Compounding Pharmacies' (*Death Penalty Information Center*) <https://deathpenaltyinfo.org/executions/methods-of-execution/lethal-injection/compounding-pharmacies> accessed 16 October 2025.

84 J Payne and others, 'Quantification of Sodium Pentobarbital Residues from Equine Mortality Compost Piles' (2015) 93 Journal of Animal Science 1824.

85 Chasity Bagsby and others, 'Stability of Pentobarbital in Soil' (2018) 53 Journal of Environmental Science and Health, Part B 207.

86 Amanda M Kaiser and others, 'Secondary Pentobarbital Poisoning in Two Dogs: A Cautionary Tale' (2010) 22 Journal of Veterinary Diagnostic Investigation 632; Office of Regulatory Affairs, 'Evanger's Pet Food and Against the Grain Voluntarily Recalls Additional Products Out of Abundance of Caution Due to Potential Adulteration with Pentobarbital' (6 June 2019) <https://www.fda.gov/safety/recalls-market-withdrawals-safety-alerts/evangers-pet-food-and-against-grain-voluntarily-recalls-additional-products-out-abundance-caution> accessed 31 July 2025.

87 Carla CCR de Carvalho and M Manuela R da Fonseca, 'The Remarkable *Rhodococcus erythropolis*' (2005) 67 Applied Microbiology and Biotechnology 715, 715.

water-fearing anthropogenic chemicals, including those used for plastics, pesticides, petroleum, and pharmaceuticals.[88] Its resilience as a solvent-tolerant microbe has made it a popular bioremediator for industry, which has used the bacteria to break down environmental waste and as a catalyst for synthesising new profit-generating compounds.[89]

Despite its many industrial uses and benefits, *R. erythropolis* has also been identified as an opportunistic pathogen, capable of causing disease when exposed to humans and animals.[90] Consequently, the human relationship with *R. erythropolis* is complicated. Anthropogenic chemicals have significantly contributed to creating the contaminated and polluted environments that are so crucial to its survival, adaptation, and expansion as colonies. Their flourishing has become essential to the ethical functioning of human industry. But we pay a price for creating and capitalising on these conditions. The more hostile and contaminated *R. erythropolis*' environments become, the greater their adaptive recalcitrance and resilience, the greater their allure for profit-driven industry, and the more hazardous the effects on human health. Indeed, these costs are borne by some groups more than others, who are forced to live and work around these "landscapes of exposure", and usually fall along the divides of race and class.[91] It is not a stretch to say that we live in a toxic regime where how we punish has significant consequences for life and nonlife outside the immediate zones of punitive influence. The afterlife of Pentobarbital shows how chemicals can transcend their purpose, quietly reshaping ecosystems they were never meant to touch. Punitive chemicalities contribute to lifecycles, political economies, and forms of being that remain under-explored and, quite frankly, un-captured by traditional studies of capital punishment.

Death Penalty in the Chemosphere

The drugs that states use to kill their condemned circulate within a toxic regime that has far-reaching consequences for human and nonhuman communities beyond the institutional setting that most legal accounts of capital punishment centralise. Since the original design of the lethal injection, barbiturates featured as the obvious choice for an anaesthetic. Low-cost, fast-acting, and readily available, barbiturates were frequently used in medical settings as pre-surgery sedatives and in veterinary medicine to euthanise

88 de Carvalho and da Fonseca (n 87).

89 Ibid., 715.

90 Hisashi Baba and others, 'First Case of Bloodstream Infection Caused by *Rhodococcus erythropolis*' (2009) 47 Journal of Clinical Microbiology 2667.

91 P O'Hare, 'Landfill Life and the Many Lives of Landfills' in Zsuzsa Gille and Josh Lepawsky (eds.), Chapter 5, *The Routledge Handbook of Waste Studies* (Routledge 2021); Michelle Murphy, 'Chemical Regimes of Living' (2008) 13 Environmental History 695; Jody A Roberts and Nancy Langston, 'Toxic Bodies/Toxic Environments: An Interdisciplinary Forum [Introduction]' (2008) 13 Environmental History 629.

animals.[92] In the context of the death penalty, concerns about its toxicity and addictive potential were minimal. If anything, their poisonous nature was seen as an advantage.

But as I argued in the previous chapter, toxicity is not an inherent property of discrete substances. It is a relational intensity, brought out by the ecological conditions under which different agencies intra-act. Pentothal, for instance, was a beneficial reagent until it was forced into wartime conditions. Administered to haemorrhaging bodies, Pentothal's behaviour changed. The events at Pearl Harbour illustrated that neither Pentothal nor human bodies are static and inert substances; they are ecologically co-emergent. Their surrounding environment enables and constrains their propensities and potentials.

In the first part of this chapter, I examined what it means to live in a chemosphere, where human "being" cannot be easily disentangled from the chemical relationalities that facilitate and inhibit the body's capacity to act. We are a "chemical species" living in a chemically-mediated world, and our chemical existence must inform our ethics. To that end, it is crucial that we acknowledge the limits of human science, which requires stable substances and passive environments in order to make predictions about how things are likely to interact. Science itself – as I argued earlier in this chapter when I compared Mendeleev and Lavoisier's conceptualisation of chemical elements – is inherently political. It represents one way of organising a disordered and chaotic world, arranging it into neat categories to enable us to interpret the past and anticipate the future. Science operates as a framework through which humans attempt to render natural processes intelligible and, at times, subject to control. Just as the discoveries of radioactivity decay and nuclear fission unsettled the foundational assumptions of chemistry, what we know about the natural world is shaped not only by available technologies, but by the instruments and experimental frameworks through which the natural world is made observable. They do not simply reveal reality; they shape what can be seen, measured, and understood. Science, therefore, does not provide purely objective or universal truths, but produces knowledge that is historically and materially situated.

I opened this chapter with a discussion about the law and how legal discourse about capital punishment is dominated by questions about the pain and suffering of prisoners, and whether the chemical combinations being used for the death penalty are capable of killing with efficiency and certainty. As a natural product that has been engineered to fit human interests, the lab-crafted configuration of the chemicals being used is never up for debate. It is clear from the courts' rulings that the "science" of their effectiveness is something that should be left up to scientists to debate and resolve, no matter that

92 Ty Alper, 'Anesthetizing the Public Conscience: Lethal Injection and Animal Euthanasia' (2008) 35 Fordham Urban Law Journal 817, 817–8.

the protocols were established by individuals who clearly did not appreciate the complexities of chemical relationality and have been tinkered with and customised by bureaucrats who have no specialised scientific training. When confronted with failed executions, the courts have explained them away as either the outcome of rectifiable human error or as natural accidents that are unlikely to be repeated. In either case, we are given the impression that the "botched" execution is an oddity, and this view persists despite the fact that, in recent years, more than a third of executions using this method have failed in some manner.[93]

Murphy notes that, within dominant scientific and regulatory discussions about chemical exposure and toxicity, two entrenched epistemic "habits" emerge. According to the first, chemicals are envisaged as discrete, self-contained, and ontologically stable molecules. They are flattened into abstract diagrams, purified of context, history, and affect.[94] Chemistry creates and sustains this image of chemicals as natural objects, with neatly bounded structures and universally identifiable properties. Within this framework, chemical exposure is treated as a purely technical issue, something measurable, controllable, and ethically neutral. This approach is especially evident in politico-legal discourse around the death penalty. In this context, the chemicals used for lethal injection are rhetorically separated from the bodies they affect. Execution protocols, for example, simply instruct prisons to administer a "lethal substance or substances" in a "quantity sufficient to cause death".[95] The actual identity of the chemicals no longer matters; what matters is their capacity to kill. In this way, barbiturates simply become molecular tools emptied of moral weight, as if their participation in death is merely procedural or instrumental. Barbiturate activity is divested of normative significance. Severed from ecosystem, bodies, and biopolitical function, barbiturates are imagined as having no life beyond their use as death instruments.

Recently, the manufacturers of Pentothal and Pentobarbital have stopped providing these drugs to correctional institutions, partially as a result of international pressures from death penalty abolitionists, and partially because their production is no longer profitable given that their clinical use is being replaced with less toxic drugs like benzodiazepines. It appears that the death penalty industry alone is insufficient to sustain the profit-driven interests of big Pharma. In their absence, correctional institutions have revised their protocols to allow them to purchase death penalty drugs from compounding pharmacies.[96]

93 Elizabeth Haigh, 'Why US Activists Have Declared 2022 the "Year of the Botched Execution"' (*Jurist News*, 20 April 2023) <https://www.jurist.org/features/2023/04/20/explainer-why-us-activists-have-declared-2022-the-year-of-the-botched-execution/> accessed 8 October 2025.

94 Murphy, 'Alterlife and Decolonial Relations' (n 35) 495.

95 'IGA | 2024 Indiana Code' (n 17) IC 35-38-6-1, Section 1(a)(1).

96 Dana E Sherman, 'Compounded Drugs, Experimentation, and Baze: Time for a Better Solution Notes' (2015) 47 Columbia Human Rights Law Review 200.

Compounding pharmacies create customised drugs by combining, mixing, and altering pharmaceutical ingredients to produce the pharmacological results desired. This is problematic for several reasons. First, as Denno explains, compounding pharmacies are not federally regulated by the United States Food and Drug Administration and are therefore not bound by the strict manufacturing standards that commercial manufacturers are required to follow.[97] But more importantly, compounding pharmacies obscure the ethical and ontological entanglements between chemicals, bodies, and institutions of power by rendering chemicals interchangeable and reducing them to purely anthropogenic functions. Operating in ethical grey areas – employing hazardous manufacturing procedures, selling contaminated medicines, and committing a host of health and safety violations – it is questionable whether these corporate entities can guarantee the material specificity (e.g. purity, stability, origin) of the drugs they sell.[98]

Compounding pharmacies are sites where chemical agency is suppressed in favour of instrumental, state-driven goals, and where the commodification of biopower sits at odds with ethical demands to remain accountable for how we punish. The number of failed executions has risen with the use of compounded chemicals,[99] and the courts have temporarily stayed executions for death row inmates in cases where the state's secrecy laws have made it impossible to determine the purity of the compounded drugs being obtained.[100] But the whole concept of "chemical purity" is itself a false narrative, mobilised by the sciences, supported by sociopolitical infrastructures, and generally deployed to make us feel more at ease about the prospective turns, probabilistic tendencies of chemical agency and volatility. As Latour and Woolgar observe, processes of purification rely on context-specific standards and technological capabilities.[101] This means that what counts as "chemical purity" is not universal but politically charged and historically contingent. Often framed as a scientific or technical ideal, purity narratives reflect a colonising logic in terms of how they conceive matter as something that can be isolated, purified, and stabilised for human use. They also imply that matter is only valuable when it is pure, usable, and predictable. Impurity thus stands in for recalcitrant

97 Denno (n 18) 1332.

98 'Missouri Executed 17 Prisoners With Drugs Secretly Obtained From "High-Risk" Pharmacy Cited for Hazardous Practices' (Death Penalty Information Center) <https://deathpenaltyinfo.org/missouri-executed-17-prisoners-with-drugs-secretly-obtained-from-high-risk-pharmacy-cited-for-hazardous-practices> accessed 30 July 2025.

99 Wade Goodwyn, 'Botched Lethal Injection Executions Reignite Death Penalty Debate' *NPR* (2015) <https://www.npr.org/2015/01/06/375399560/botched-lethal-injection-executions-reignite-death-penalty-debate> accessed 8 October 2025.

100 *Hill v Owens* (2013) Ga. 380, 738 S.E.2d 292 56 (Ga).

101 Bruno Latour and Steve Woolgar, *Laboratory Life: The Construction of Scientific Facts* (Princeton University Press 1986) 59.

matter, matter that refuses to comply with human design. It becomes a way to suppress material agency and present matter as passive.

To focus on chemical purity also draws attention away from the ongoing entanglement between incarcerated bodies, chemical agency, and the contaminated ecologies of the prison. This brings me back to the second epistemic habit that Murphy identifies within existing discussions about chemical exposure, and that is its focus on damage-based narratives. Damage-based approaches to toxicity rely on scientific and regulatory frameworks that define "damage" on the basis of measurable and quantifiable harm or injury to individual bodies. Toxicity is thus only acknowledged after measurable damage has occurred and once it meets institutional or scientific standards of evidence. For Murphy, damage-based approaches overlook the broader social, economic, and colonial contexts in which chemical toxicity operates, and thus do not adequately capture cumulative, cross-generational exposure because a specific harm cannot be easily isolated and attributed to a single cause.

By treating toxicity as an isolated "event" rather than ongoing structural processes, damage-based toxicity diverts attention from the broader "*infrastructures* of chemical violence in the world" to focus more heavily on its "molecular manifestations in bodies and communities already living in hostile conditions".[102] To thus connect the damage that bodies undergo as part of the execution process to the impurity of the chemicals being used by correctional facilities is to miss how systemic, slow violence accumulates and transforms bodily vulnerability. Damage-based narratives reinforce normative assumptions about bodies, but bodies in prison – as Chapter 3 showed – are not the same as bodies that are "free". They are subject to different traumas and deprivations – overcrowding, medical neglect, malnutrition, stress, and chemical exposure[103] – all of which ensure that the chemical compositions of bodies-in-prison are remarkably different to the standard body of laboratory science. This does not even begin to account for the different pre-carceral contexts that shape the bodies of the marginalised and impoverished populations that disproportionately end up in prison.

In that sense, the prison itself becomes a site of material conditioning. It has a part to play in how bodies respond pharmacologically and materially to chemical exposure. Purity narratives neglect the systemic structures which

102 Murphy, 'Alterlife and Decolonial Relations' (n 35) 496.

103 Mark T Berg and others, 'Losing Years Doing Time: Incarceration Exposure and Accelerated Biological Aging among African American Adults' (2021) 62 Journal of Health and Social Behavior 460; Kacie McCoy Daugherty, 'Synthetic Sanity: The Ethics and Legality of Using Psychotropic Medications to Render Death Row Inmates Competent for Execution Comment' (2000) 17 Journal of Contemporary Health Law and Policy 715; Marie Mulvey Roberts, *Writing for Their Lives: Death Row U.S.A.* (University of Illinois Press 2007); Cedric Michel, 'Death Row Inmates: Housing and Management Issues' in Kimberly D Dodson (ed), *Routledge Handbook on Offenders with Special Needs* (Routledge 2018).

condition the body itself, as an *ecology*. Framing capital punishment in this way makes clearer how failed executions are not technological and procedural failures, but symptoms of state-produced entanglements between structural harm and chemical action. Rather than viewing the incarcerated body as a neutral site for state-administered toxicity, we must attend to the material histories that condition the body's reactivity to administered chemicals. The idea of chemical purity and damage-based toxicity presumes a stable, predictable (human) agent into which stable, predictable chemicals are being injected. Yet, within the overcrowded, medically neglected, malnourished conditions of carceral institutions, bodies are already chemically saturated, weakened, and altered. These are not "failed" subjects, nor "impure" drugs; rather, their entanglement reveals the fragility of purity itself, and the violence of the fantasy that chemical substances act uniformly across all bodies. In clinging to the illusion of chemical precision and the universality of the human body, death penalty states persist in navigating a fraught boundary between humane and inhumane execution. Both penal institutions, and the juridical machinery that sustain them, are mistaken in their belief that the act of killing can ever be rendered fully humane or absolutely engineered.

Works Cited

Affairs O of R, 'Evanger's Pet Food and Against the Grain Voluntarily Recalls Additional Products Out of Abundance of Caution Due to Potential Adulteration with Pentobarbital' (6 June 2019) <https://www.fda.gov/safety/recalls-market-withdrawals-safety-alerts/evangers-pet-food-and-against-grain-voluntarily-recalls-additional-products-out-abundance-caution> accessed 31 July 2025.

Agard-Jones V, 'Bodies in the System' (2013) 17 Small Axe 182.

Alaimo S, *Bodily Natures: Science, Environment, and the Material Self* (Indiana University Press 2010).

Alaimo S, *Exposed* (University of Minnesota Press 2016).

Alper T, 'Anesthetizing the Public Conscience: Lethal Injection and Animal Euthanasia' (2008) 35 Fordham Urban Law Journal 817.

'As Lethal Injection Turns Forty, States Botch a Record Number of Executions' (*Death Penalty Information Center*, 2022) <https://deathpenaltyinfo.org/news/as-lethal-injection-turns-forty-states-botch-a-record-number-of-executions> accessed 8 August 2024.

Baba H and others, 'First Case of Bloodstream Infection Caused by *Rhodococcus erythropolis*' (2009) 47 Journal of Clinical Microbiology 2667.

Bagsby C and others, 'Stability of Pentobarbital in Soil' (2018) 53 Journal of Environmental Science and Health, Part B 207.

Balayannis A and Garnett E, 'Chemical Kinship: Interdisciplinary Experiments with Pollution' (2020) 6 Catalyst: Feminism, Theory, Technoscience 1.

Barad K, *Meeting the Universe Halfway: Quantum Physics and the Entanglement of Matter and Meaning* (Duke University Press 2007).

Bennett J, *Vibrant Matter: A Political Ecology of Things* (Duke University Press 2010).

Bennetts FE, 'Thiopentone Anaesthesia at Pearl Harbour' (1995) 75 British Journal of Anaesthesia 366.

Berg MT and others, 'Losing Years Doing Time: Incarceration Exposure and Accelerated Biological Aging among African American Adults' (2021) 62 Journal of Health and Social Behavior 460.

Berger E, 'Lethal Injection and the Problem of Constitutional Remedies' (2008) 27 Yale Law & Policy Review 259.

Borg MJ and Radelet ML, 'On Botched Executions' in Peter Hodgkinson and William A Schabas (eds), *Capital Punishment: Strategies for Abolition* (Cambridge University Press 2004)..

Brazer DS, 'Lethal Paralytics and the Censorship of Suffering' (2023) 57 Columbia Journal of Law and Social Problems 1.

Brönmark C and Hansson L-A, 'Chemical Communication in Aquatic Systems: An Introduction' (2000) 88 Oikos 103.

Burdick AS, 'The Manufacture of Synthetic Medicinal Chemicals in America*' (1922) 11 The Journal of the American Pharmaceutical Association (1912) 98.

Cardwell E, 'Moral Economies of Life and Death: Agricultural Improvement, Imperialism, and Chemical Kinships with Reactive Nitrogen' (2023) 9 Catalyst: Feminism, Theory, Technoscience <https://catalystjournal.org/index.php/catalyst/article/view/38415> accessed 24 September 2024.

Chambers CD, Brill L and Inciardi JA, 'Barbiturate Use, Misuse and Abuse' (1972) 2 Journal of Drug Issues 15.

'Compounding Pharmacies' (Death Penalty Information Center) <https://deathpenaltyinfo.org/executions/methods-of-execution/lethal-injection/compounding-pharmacies> accessed 16 October 2025.

Costandi M, 'Life after Death: The Science of Human Decomposition' *The Guardian* (5 May 2015) <https://www.theguardian.com/science/neurophilosophy/2015/may/05/life-after-death> accessed 22 July 2025.

Cozanitis DA, 'One Hundred Years of Barbiturates and Their Saint' (2004) 97 Journal of the Royal Society of Medicine 594.

Crider HD, 'The Story of the Diamond' (1924) 9 The American Midland Naturalist 176.

Crowhurst JA, 'The Legacy of the Anaesthesia Events at Pearl Harbor, 7th December 1941' (2016) 24 Journal of Military and Veteran's Health 52.

Daugherty KM, 'Synthetic Sanity: The Ethics and Legality of Using Psychotropic Medications to Render Death Row Inmates Competent for Execution Comment' (2000) 17 Journal of Contemporary Health Law and Policy 715.

de Carvalho CCCR and da Fonseca MMR, 'The Remarkable *Rhodococcus erythropolis*' (2005) 67 Applied Microbiology and Biotechnology 715.

Dennis F, 'Chemical Species: The Art and Politics of Living with(out) Drugs after Addiction' (2023) 18 BioSocieties 545.

Denno DW, 'The Lethal Injection Quandary: How Medicine Dismantled the Death Penalty' (2007) 76 Fordham L. Rev. 49.

Denno DW, 'Lethal Injection Chaos Post-Baze' (2013) 102 Georgetown Law Journal 1331.

Eckel WP, Ross B and Isensee RK, 'Pentobarbital Found in Ground Water' (1993) 31 Groundwater 801.

Fine B, 'Coal, Diamonds and Oil: Toward a Conparative Theory of Mining? *' (1994) 6 Review of Political Economy 279.

Fulkerson A and Suttmoeller M, 'Current Issues Involving Lethal Injection' (2008) 21 Criminal Justice Studies 271.

Glatt MM, 'The Abuse of Barbiturates in the United Kingdom' [1962] UNODC (United Nations Office on Drugs and Crime) <//www.unodc.org/unodc/en/data-and-analysis/bulletin/bulletin_1962-01-01_2_page004.html> accessed 29 July 2025.

Goodwyn W, 'Botched Lethal Injection Executions Reignite Death Penalty Debate' *NPR* (2015) <https://www.npr.org/2015/01/06/375399560/botched-lethal-injection-executions-reignite-death-penalty-debate> accessed 8 October 2025.

Haigh E, 'Why US Activists Have Declared 2022 the "Year of the Botched Execution"' (*Jurist News*, 20 April 2023) <https://www.jurist.org/features/2023/04/20/explainer-why-us-activists-have-declared-2022-the-year-of-the-botched-execution/> accessed 8 October 2025.

Halford FJ, 'A Critique of Intravenous Anesthesia in War Surgery' (1943) 4 Anesthesiology 67.

Hauser CJ, 'Preclinical Models of Traumatic, Hemorrhagic Shock' (2005) 24 Shock 24.

Helmreich S, 'Elementary Forms of Elementary Forms: Old, New, and Wavy' in Dimitris Papadopoulos, Maria Puig de la Bellacasa and Natasha Myers (eds), *Reactivating Elements: Chemistry, Ecology, Practice* (Duke University Press 2021).

Hill JF and Olson V, 'The Chemical Kinship of Stony Entities' <http://juliefhill.co.uk> accessed 25 July 2025.

'IGA | 2024 Indiana Code' <https://iga.in.gov/laws/2024/ic/titles/35#35-38-6-1> accessed 27 July 2025.

Kaiser AM and others, 'Secondary Pentobarbital Poisoning in Two Dogs: A Cautionary Tale' (2010) 22 Journal of Veterinary Diagnostic Investigation 632.

Kevorkian J, 'Medicine, Ethics, and Execution by Lethal Injection' (1985) 4 Medicine and Law 307.

Kuznetski (Née Tofantšuk) J and Alaimo S, 'Transcorporeality: An Interview with Stacy Alaimo' (2020) 11 Ecozon@: European Journal of Literature, Culture and Environment 137.

Lain CB, *Secrets of the Killing State: The Untold Story of Lethal Injection* (New York University Press 2025).

Latour B and Woolgar S, *Laboratory Life: The Construction of Scientific Facts* (Princeton University Press 1986).

Lavoisier A, *Elements of Chemistry: In a New Systematic Order, Containing All the Modern Discoveries* (Robert Kerr tr, Fifth Edinburgh Edition, Evert Duyckinck 1806).

Levi P, *The Periodic Table* (Penguin 1986).

López-Muñoz F, Ucha-Udabe R and Alamo C, 'The History of Barbiturates a Century after Their Clinical Introduction' (2005) 1 Neuropsychiatric Disease and Treatment 329.

McGreal C, 'Lethal Injection Drug Production Ends in the US' *The Guardian* (23 January 2011) <https://www.theguardian.com/world/2011/jan/23/lethal-injection-sodium-thiopental-hospira> accessed 16 October 2025.

Michel C, 'Death Row Inmates: Housing and Management Issues' in Kimberly D Dodson (ed), *Routledge Handbook on Offenders with Special Needs* (Routledge 2018).

'Missouri Executed 17 Prisoners With Drugs Secretly Obtained From "High-Risk" Pharmacy Cited for Hazardous Practices' (Death Penalty Information Center) <https://deathpenaltyinfo.org/missouri-executed-17-prisoners-with-drugs-secretly-obtained-from-high-risk-pharmacy-cited-for-hazardous-practices> accessed 30 July 2025.

Murphy M, 'Alterlife and Decolonial Relations' (2017) 32 Cultural Anthropology 494.

Murphy M, 'Chemical Regimes of Living' (2008) 13 Environmental History 695.

Murphy M, 'Current Book in Progress' (13 November 2007) <https://michellemurphy.net/technoscience-meets-biopolitics/> accessed 30 July 2025.

Neal MJ, *Medical Pharmacology at a Glance* (Proquest Ebook Central, John Wiley & Sons 2015).

Neilson S, 'Lethal Injection Drugs' Efficacy And Availability For Federal Executions' *NPR* (26 July 2019) <https://www.npr.org/2019/07/26/745722219/lethal-injection-drugs-efficacy-and-availability-for-federal-executions> accessed 16 October 2025.

O'Hare P, 'Landfill Life and the Many Lives of Landfills' in Zsuzsa Gille and Josh Lepawsky (eds.), Chapter 5, *The Routledge Handbook of Waste Studies* (Routledge 2021).

Ortiz E and Brooks A, 'In Texas, New Details about Its Execution Drug Underscore a Closely Guarded Secret' (*NBC News*, 14 October 2025) <https://www.nbcnews.com/news/us-news/texas-new-details-execution-drug-underscore-closely-guarded-secret-rcna236168> accessed 16 October 2025.

Papadopoulos D, 'Chemicals, Ecology, and Reparative Justice' in Dimitris Papadopoulos, Maria Puig de la Bellacasa and Natasha Myers (eds), *Reactivating Elements: Chemistry, Ecology, Practice* (Duke University Press 2021).

Payne J and others, 'Quantification of Sodium Pentobarbital Residues from Equine Mortality Compost Piles' (2015) 93 Journal of Animal Science 1824.

Priest SM and Geisbuhler TP, 'Injectable Sodium Pentobarbital: Stability at Room Temperature' (2015) 76 Journal of Pharmacological and Toxicological Methods 38.

Roberts JA and Langston N, 'Toxic Bodies/Toxic Environments: An Interdisciplinary Forum [Introduction]' (2008) 13 Environmental History 629.

Roberts MM, *Writing for Their Lives: Death Row U.S.A.* (University of Illinois Press 2007).

Sarat A, *Gruesome Spectacles: Botched Executions and America's Death Penalty* (Stanford University Press 2016).

Sarat A, *Lethal Injection and the False Promise of Humane Execution* (Stanford University Press 2022).

Schelling FWJ von and Peterson KR, *First Outline of a System of the Philosophy of Nature* (State University of New York Press 2004).

Schiestl FP, 'The Evolution of Floral Scent and Insect Chemical Communication' (2010) 13 Ecology Letters 643.

Schultz T, 'Europe Fights the Death Penalty — with Drugs' (*The World from PRX*, 2 August 2016) <https://theworld.org/stories/2016/08/02/europe-fights-death-penalty-drugs> accessed 9 May 2025.

Shapiro N, 'Attuning to the Chemosphere: Domestic Formaldehyde, Bodily Reasoning, and the Chemical Sublime' (2015) 30 Cultural Anthropology 368.

Sherman DE, 'Compounded Drugs, Experimentation, and Baze: Time for a Better Solution Notes' (2015) 47 Columbia Human Rights Law Review 200.

Simon J and Bensaude-Vincent B, *Chemistry: The Impure Science (Second Edition)* (World Scientific Publishing Company 2012).

'So Long as They Die: Lethal Injections in the United States: I. Development of Lethal Injection Protocols' (*Human Rights Watch*, 2006) <https://www.hrw.org/reports/2006/us0406/3.htm> accessed 25 July 2025.

Tremoleda JL and others, 'Modeling Acute Traumatic Hemorrhagic Shock Injury: Challenges and Guidelines for Preclinical Studies' (2017) 48 Shock 610.

Ueda H, Kikuta Y and Matsuda K, 'Plant Communication: Mediated by Individual or Blended VOCs?' (2012) 7 Plant Signaling & Behavior 222.

Urell A, 'Lethal Injections Cause Suffocation and Severe Pain, Autopsies Show' (*Equal Justice Initiative*, 22 September 2020) <https://eji.org/news/lethal-injections-cause-suffocation-and-severe-pain-autopsies-show/> accessed 31 August 2025.

Zain ME, 'Impact of Mycotoxins on Humans and Animals' (2011) 15 Journal of Saudi Chemical Society 129.

Zencirci N and others, 'Crystal Polymorphs of Barbital: News about a Classic Polymorphic System' (2014) 11 Molecular Pharmaceutics 338.

Zivot JB, Edgar MA and Lubarsky DA, 'Execution by Lethal Injection: Autopsy Findings of Pulmonary Edema' (medRxiv, 27 August 2022) <https://www.medrxiv.org/content/10.1101/2022.08.24.22279183v1> accessed 5 September 2024.

Cases

Baze v Rees [2008] 553 US 35.
Bucklew v Precythe [2019] 139 S Ct 1112.
Glossip v Chandler [2021] WD Okla CIV-14-0665-F.
Glossip v Gross [2015] 135 S Ct 2726.
Hill v Owens (2013) Ga. 380, 738 S.E.2d 292 56 (Ga).
Re Ohio Execution Protocol Litigation [2014] 994 F Supp 2d 906 (SD Ohio).
Warner v Gross (2015) 776 F3d 721 (10th Cir).
Wood v Ryan [2014] 759 F 3d 1076 (9th Cir).

Conclusion

Posthuman Punishment

> Even in the anthropocene, or, especially in the anthropocene, the substance of what was once called "nature", act, interacts, and even intra-acts within, through, and around human bodies and practices. What can it mean to be human in this time when the human is something that has become sedimented in the geology of the planet? What forms of ethics and politics arise from the sense of being embedded in, exposed to, and even composed of the very stuff of a rapidly transforming material world?
>
> Stacy Alaimo, *Exposed: Environmental Politics and Pleasures in Posthuman Times*, 1.

We end the book, as we started it, with a return to the Anthropocene. While the introduction to this book urged you to use the Anthropocene as a thinking ground for ecolegal normativity, the idea of a geological epoch where humans are a central force is not without its problems. As Stacy Alaimo explains, how the Anthropocene has traditionally been imagined by the humanities and social sciences in terms of the "magnitude of the effect humans have had on the planet", redeploys the nature/culture bifurcation for new ends, and continues to uphold the "illusion that we're safely disconnected from the world we have negatively impacted". Thinking in these terms, she cautions, "may give us a false sense of power that shields us from considering differential human vulnerability. We are *always part of the world we have affected*, and many different groups of people…are being harmed by the 'Anthropocene'".[1]

One response to this critique has been the reimagining of human life through connective channels that decentre both the human figure and Nature (in the more traditional sense), focusing instead on global capital flows. Capitalocene speaks of a "world-ecology of capital, power, nature" in which exercises of oppression are intimately connected with capitalist accumulation,

1 Julia Kuznetski (née Kuznetski (Nee Tofantsuk and Stacy Alaimo, 'Transcorporeality: An Interview with Stacy Alaimo' (2020) 11 Ecozon@: European Journal of Literature, Culture and Environment 137, 138–9.

DOI: 10.4324/9781003367567-6

extractivism, and how best to acquire "Cheap Nature".[2] But the Capitalocene also does not, as Haraway explains, engender care for and responsibility towards other worlds, human and nonhuman.[3] The reality is that humans live on this damaged planet, in conjunction with, alongside, and through geological, chemical, microbial, hydrological, and technological worlds a many, and to think about human institutions, practice, and law without care for and responsibility towards other worlds limits our ability to imagine a world that is not all hope or despair. To do this, we must, Haraway appeals, "make kin with", "reworld, reimagine, relive, and reconnect with each other, in multispecies well-being".[4] This multilayered, multispecies, entangled way of thinking about living and dying on a shared planet ushers in a timespace that Haraway dubs the "Chthulucene", made up of "ongoing multispecies stories and practices of becoming-with in times that remain at stake, in precarious times, in which the world is not finished and the sky has not fallen – yet".[5]

Punishment has sought to bring to light the ways in which human life is embedded in natural processes. Humans live through and amidst worlds that are not only essential to our survival as a species, but also critical to our politics. To envision this relationship as one of human domination is not only self-centred and naïve, but perilously reductive. While scholars have explored how environmental forces intersect with race, class, gender, and Indigeneity,[6] far less attention has been paid to how these same forces shape the embodied realities of criminalised populations – those already positioned as disposable, deviant, and beyond moral community. This neglect reflects a broader failure to reckon with how life deemed criminal is also exposed to intensifying forms of ecological and systemic precarity.

While the preceding chapters have sought to centre fungal and chemical agency, I hope it was clear that this agency, this power to act and affect, is relational. Fungi and chemicals express creativity and purposiveness *through* the natural processes of adaptation, growth, decay, mutation, and expansion in intra-action with their human and nonhuman environment. Obviously, the clear implication here is that humans do not stand apart from nature; they

2 Jason W Moore, *Anthropocene or Capitalocene?: Nature, History, and the Crisis of Capitalism* (PM Press 2016).

3 Donna Haraway, *Staying with the Trouble: Making Kin in the Chthulucene* (Duke University Press 2016) 50.

4 Ibid., 50–1.

5 Ibid., 55.

6 Gwyn Kirk, 'Ecofeminism and Environmental Justice: Bridges across Gender, Race, and Class' (1997) 18 Frontiers: A Journal of Women Studies 2; Susan L Cutter, 'Race, Class and Environmental Justice' (1995) 19 Progress in Human Geography 111; Sheila Foster, 'Race(Ial)Matters: The Quest for Environmental Justice' (1993) 20 Ecology Law Quarterly 721; Diana Lewis and others, 'Linking Land Displacement and Environmental Dispossession to Mi'kmaw Health and Well-Being: Culturally Relevant Place-Based Interpretive Frameworks Matter' (2021) 65 Canadian Geographies / Géographies canadiennes 66.

are nature, and thus they, too, express their agency in intra-action with these entities and forces. The human and nonhuman world mutually constitute one another; they are enabled and constrained by each other's patterns of behaviour. In the framing that Davies uses, human norms are emergent with the normativity of Nature.

Consequently, the ecological view of punishment that I have sought to develop over the course of this book is one which considers Nature as a political force in its own right, rather than a passive and mechanical backdrop for human politics. In "making kin" with fungi and chemicals, Chapters 3 and 4 have jointly exposed some significant, but previously concealed, relations of power that have bearing on the exercise and experience of punitive control. It may not be immediately obvious that the politics of settler colonialism, Indigenous dispossession, white supremacy, capitalist extractivism, corporatism, and industrial agriculture impose social order *materially*, by conditioning the very constituting matter of human bodies. Nature resists the spatio-temporal logics of western epistemology, making it difficult to accurately trace or map the ecological impact of human activity and politics. Over time, these ecological iterations become "normalised", such that phenomena that might previously have been recognised as pollution, disease, disability, impurity or contamination are simply shrugged off as a "common fact of contemporary life". These burdens and exposures are not evenly distributed across contemporary society and are disproportionately shouldered by the most marginalised populations. Sometimes, these exposures are overshadowed by corporate interests masked as being in the general public good.[7] But they are exposures that have relevance for ethical debate about how to best live alongside this multispecies world.

In the context of punishment, the ethical questions raised by the Anthropocene call for a reimagining of both discourse and practice, shifting away from institutional, human-centred approaches and towards ecological frameworks that recognise the material networks in which humans are entangled and through which they become. To this end, this book offers three critical new pathways for rethinking punishment in the Anthropocene. The first is that it raises questions about the meaning and exercise of toxicity: how are we to understand toxic fungi, toxic chemicals, toxic practices, and what kind of subjectivities arise when we think about toxicity as an inescapable facet of the human condition? What role should this framing of toxicity as relationality play within mainstream punishment discourse?

Second, it brings into sharper relief the trans-corporeal nature of ecological harm. The effects of fungal infection and chemical exposure extend beyond the bodies and institutions with which they have direct contact. Chemicals and microbials of all kinds are capable of crossing corporeal boundaries, seeping

7 See my discussion of *R. erythropolis* in Chapter 4, a contaminant-adapted microbe that was used by industry to break down environmental waste.

into nature, fusing with new elements, forces, and agencies, and creating new subjectivities. These material flows are continuously "cycling through living systems", blurring the boundaries between life and nonlife.[8] Their effects can be transcribed in new bodies through epigenetic transfer and reactivated in old bodies living under new conditions. Chemical and fungal life resist containment within the linear, anthropocentric logics of western epistemology. Their temporalities and spatialities exceed simple cause-and-effect reasoning, unfolding instead through dispersed, entangled, and nonhuman rhythms of becoming.[9] What is ethical punishment in light of these trans-corporeal mappings of harm, culpability, and responsibility?

Third, this book rethinks what Davies terms the "pathological" by foregrounding the norm-generating force of "accidents", those seemingly chaotic, violent, or random events typically dismissed as socio-politically irrelevant. Pathological events are simultaneously destructive and transformative; they fracture familiar identities, structures, and meanings while giving rise to new configurations of order. Toxicity, trans-corporeality, and pathology emerge as sites of material and affective reconfiguring, generating alternative modes of being and becoming with normative implications for human life. Each of these dimensions of what I will call *posthuman punishment* is explored in more detail in the sections that follow.

Intoxicated Becomings

To call something "toxic" is to define it in terms of the harm it poses to human-centred life. Toxicity is typically imagined as an inherent property of a substance, a *toxicant*, that exists independently of the bodies it affects. By tracing the material histories of both Cocci and barbiturates, I argue that this view oversimplifies the reality. As materials that circulate through other organisms, water, air, soil, and flesh, and altered by technology and human practice, the lifecycles of both materials reveal how toxicity is not inherent, but emergent, arising through ecological intra-actions. Toxicity is a relational phenomenon that materialises within assemblages of bodies, things, technologies, and events.

In Chapter 3, I discuss the relational toxicity of Cocci by tracing how industrial agriculture produces weather events that force Cocci to take on new forms (moving from mycelium to spore to spherule), perform new deeds (detach, disperse, take root, embed, multiply), and how these movements

8 Margaret Davies, *EcoLaw: Legality, Life, and the Normativity of Nature* (Taylor & Francis 2022) 78.

9 Karen Barad, 'Troubling Time/s and Ecologies of Nothingness: Re-Turning, Re-Membering, and Facing the Incalculable' (2018) 92 New Formations: a Journal of Culture/Theory/Politics 56, 59–60.

become parasitic only once this organism is introduced to the hostile climates of human and animal bodies. Similarly, in Chapter 4, I discuss how barbiturates are not inherently toxic, but that they become so by way of technological interventions that alter their atomic structure and are introduced to human bodies using specific modes of delivery and in specific concentrations. As the example of Pentothal's use during Pearl Harbor illustrates, it is the specific conditions of the host body that can transform a therapeutic barbiturate into a toxicant. Toxicity here is not an inherent property, but an effect that emerges through the entangled relations between chemical, body, and context.

Equally, toxicity is not simply a material fact, but also an epistemic phenomenon, one that materialises through the privileged discourses of endemicity and purity, the enacted technologies of skin tests and spectrometers, and the mobilised knowledge practices of chemistry, epidemiology, and mycology. It is immanent to the practice of medical practitioners, epidemiologists, and chemists as they render certain entities visible and interpret their interplays in ways that matter for human life. These vantage points are not neutral, but entangled with political, cultural, and economic forces.[10]

Within the context of punishment, these chemical and fungal regimes of power are structurally situated and historically dispersed. Toxicity is ambient; it is hard to detect and unevenly experienced across racialised, gendered and classed communities. For bodies in prison, toxicity has become a routine facet of a life lived in overcrowded, malnourished, and chemically saturated conditions. So much so that one cannot possibly speak about the ethics of lethal injection or the issue of prisoner disease and their effects without considering the toxic regime under which imprisoned bodies persist. Judgements of cruel and unusual punishment that focus narrowly on institutional or individual responsibility risk overlooking the intertwined material forces shaping these harms. Responsibility cannot be confined to those directly poisoned or those who do the poisoning, for toxicants dissolve such boundaries.[11] Instead, responsibility is systemic and distributed across the infrastructures of industrial capitalism and corporatism, colonial and imperial expansion, and state practice, all of which reconfigure environments and bodies in their wake. This enmeshed responsibility demands an ethical reckoning with the nonhuman consequences of human action, grounded in trans-corporeal entanglements that extend beyond human subjectivity.

All this discussion of entanglement and distributed responsibility is not meant to abstract away from the embodied, lived realities of toxicity. Toxic exposure is not merely a concept; it is an experience woven into the everyday lives of those affected. In places like Avenal and PVSP, exposure to Cocci has

10 Michelle Murphy, *Sick Building Syndrome and the Problem of Uncertainty: Environmental Politics, Technoscience, and Women Workers* (Duke University Press 2006).

11 Stacy Alaimo, *Exposed* (University of Minnesota Press 2016).

reshaped the life trajectories of incarcerated people, leaving material traces that persist both during imprisonment and well beyond release. To foreground nonhuman agency and environmental entanglement is not to erase human suffering, but to situate it within the porous boundaries of bodies and landscapes, where the harms of punishment seep through lungs and soil, immune systems and carceral infrastructures. As I explain in Chapter 4, the cruelty of Pentobarbital use does not end with the pain and suffering of an inmate enduring a failed execution; it cycles through Nature in the form of contaminated waterways, soils, and rendered animal feed. Drawing on trans-corporeal ethics and the multiplicity of bodily realities, this approach insists that cruelty is not only institutional or symbolic but viscously material, lived, and shared across human and nonhuman worlds.

As Chen observes, our conversations about toxicity almost always "discuss intoxication like it's only a violent reflex of pollution, coming on like a wave from elsewhere".[12] Toxicity is rarely imagined as a common feature of human life. We are constantly looking for the pollutive "event" or agent, that singular activity or individual that we can point to and blame for the toxic result. This view of toxicity remains dominant all the while we remain entirely submerged in chemical and microbial worlds that are themselves shaped by the politics of extractivism, industrialisation, corporatisation, and capitalist overconsumption. In the absence of a singular causal event or agent, these interactions recede into the background, becoming "natural" anomalies for which humans bear no responsibility. We see clear evidence of this in both our discussions of prisoner disease and the failed execution.

For the very reason that toxicity engenders "atmospheric attunement",[13] it also becomes productive. Intoxication has its "own capabilities", its own potential to "enable taking leave of a flattening, even murderous present, to a temporal and sensory otherwise, to a place of *tolerabilility*".[14] Toxicity represents a chemical/fungal "intimacy" that operates way beyond our simplified models of cause and effect and implicates actants (and actors) outside existing punitive processes and institutions. But as Chen explains, "one of the most harmful aspects of oversight is to consider toxicity as a unipolar phenomenon – almost as if to follow its cue of exception – rather than as something *rampantly interwoven with other phenomena*".[15] In Chapters 3 and 4, I have considered how fungal and chemical toxicity are interwoven with the practices of global capitalism, industrialisation, and carceral logics and

12 Mel Y Chen, *Intoxicated: Race, Disbaility and Chemical Intimacy Across Empire* (Duke University Press 2023) 4.

13 Kathleen Stewart, 'Atmospheric Attunements' (2011) 29 Environment and Planning D: Society and Space 445; Nicholas Shapiro, 'Attuning to the Chemosphere: Domestic Formaldehyde, Bodily Reasoning, and the Chemical Sublime' (2015) 30 Cultural Anthropology 368.

14 Chen (n 12) 4.

15 Ibid., 6.

architectures, to such an extent that the attribution of legal responsibility becomes a complicated affair. The hitherto reliance on concepts like human agency, autonomy, intent, and even the idea of individual responsibility fails to address the complexities of living in a "toxic regime".[16]

As my earlier analysis of Cocci exposure indicated, toxic exposure is productive of new subjectivities. Cocci-human intra-action generated new confirgurations of life and identity, unevenly constituted within oppressive and toxic conditions of systemic racism, class oppression, state violence, and cultural dehumanisation. Immunological resilience and legal class actions are two examples of how toxic exposure generates new solidarities and forms of resistance. Toxic encounters equally alter nonhuman lives. They turn innocuous fungal spores into parasitic budding yeasts, generate new bacterial forms capable of breaking down environmental waste[17] and produce new chemical compounds with extended half-lives.[18] Anna Tsing refers to these new life-forms as expressions of "contaminated diversity":

> [C]ultural and biological ways of life that have developed [in]...collaborative adaptation to human-disturbed ecosystems. It emerges as the detritus of environmental destruction, imperial conquest, profit making, racism, and authoritarian rule—as well as creative becoming. It is not always pretty. But it is who we are and what we have as available working partners for a liveable earth.[19]

While "contamination" may reflect toxic social, political, and material conditions, it also generates unexpected forms of resistance, survival, and community-building. Contaminated diversity can be productive; it can engender both harm and hope. Mass incarceration and capital punishment thus unfold within ecologies of, what Tsing calls, "slow disturbance", ongoing environmental and social change caused by disruptive forces that produce lingering transformations over time. These produce forms of "slow violence", gradual, compounding injustices; an "attritional violence" that is "neither spectacular nor instantaneous".[20] Slow disturbances with their slow violence and contaminated

16 Dimitris Papadopoulos, 'Chemicals, Ecology, and Reparative Justice' in Dimitris Papadopoulos, Maria Puig de la Bellacasa and Natasha Myers (eds), *Reactivating Elements: Chemistry, Ecology, Practice* (Duke University Press 2021), 34–69.

17 See my discussion of *R. erythropolis* in Chapter 4.

18 See my discussion of molecular interventions that produce barbiturates with longer half-lives in Chapter 4.

19 Anna Tsing, 'Contaminated Diversity in "Slow Disturbance": Potential Collaborators for a Liveable Earth' in Gary Martin, Diana Mincyte and Ursula Münster (eds), *Why Do We Value Diversity? Biocultural Diversity in a Global Context* (RCC Perspectives 2012) 95.

20 Rob Nixon, *Slow Violence and the Environmentalism of the Poor* (Harvard University Press 2011) 2.

life forms jointly produce the new normative conditions under which we must all find ways of living together, "making kin" with contaminated diversity, and jointly devising ways to survive in these disturbed landscapes.

Trans-Corporeality

Barad observes that the Anthropocene may be a moment in our history in which "troubling time" is an ethical necessity.

> the urgency to trouble time, to shake it to its core, and to produce collective imaginaries that undo pervasive conceptions of temporality that take progress as inevitable and the past as something that has passed and is no longer *with us* is something so tangible, so visceral, that it can be felt in our individual and collective bodies.[21]

The past, I have sought to show through this book, is sedimented, not only within the layered and fossilised remains found in Nature but deep within the very molecular structures of living bodies. Human bodies are archaeological sites that reveal lives past and lives yet to come. Alaimo uses the term "trans-corporeality" to describe this environmentally embedded and entangled vision of human life, constituted through bodies porous to their surrounding world and engaged in a consistent mutual transfer of matter (chemicals, elements, water, microbes). We don't just "incorporate" the environment; we are radically changed by it, altered by the things we consume, ingest, inhale, and inject, and much of this happens without our conscious awareness and usually without our consent.[22] The environment is not something "out there", but something that lays roots deep within us, and because it is constitutive of human matter, it has significance for human life. For Barad, this trans-corporeal notion of human life casts doubt, or should cast doubt, on the "unilinear nature of time itself (the fact that only one moment exists at a time)".[23]

In moving away from this idea of bodies as sealed units, discrete objects, it becomes possible to see how our punishment practices affect broader networks across expansive space and time, influencing, among other things, mental health, dispositions to disease, toxic exposure, and even intergenerational trauma. When incarcerated people breathe polluted air, drink contaminated water, eat low-quality food, ingest compounded medicines – these materials enter the body, permeate organs, and become incorporated into molecular structures and genetic profiles. As I explained in both Chapter 3 and Chapter 4, these alterations extend beyond confinement, affecting life after release and

21 Barad (n 9) 57.

22 Stacy Alaimo, *Bodily Natures: Science, Environment, and the Material Self* (Indiana University Press 2010) 13.

23 Barad (n 9) 57.

circulating through environmental pathways to impact both human and nonhuman entities, as well as future generations through epigenomic change and slow ecological disturbance. Harms done to one body ripple through ecosystems and across time. Again, as I have already suggested above, these harms are unequally experienced by already marginalised communities, not only social groups who are disproportionately incarcerated and more likely to be given the death penalty, but also those communities that are more likely to live and work on and around polluted and poisoned lands.

So, what can a trans-corporeal view of human life add to the theory and practice of punishment? While many of the legal cases I considered framed the consequences of punishment in terms of institutional responsibility and individualised harm, trans-corporeality demands that attention be paid to systemic, epistemic, shared, and material interdependencies. It pushes for an ethic where state violence, capitalist and corporatist infrastructures, environmental degradation, and carceral practices are not isolated issues, but deeply connected, and materially enacted through and with bodies. Consequently, *how* we punish has significant implications for *where* and *whom* we punish, implications that extend far into time, across vast distances, and distributed across bodies, in ways that do not align with the vision we have of fair and just punishment. Our forms of punishment may transgress the bodily boundaries of the legally culpable, the institutional settings where we think punishment happens, and perhaps most controversially, may even traverse the temporal borders of *when* we think punishment takes place. A trans-corporeal view of punishment thus exposes punishment as materially invasive and demands that we account for the material conditions of life, and not just abstract legal categories.

At the same time, trans-corporeality *politicises* the body, designating it as a site of political struggle. We have seen the political struggle between big Pharma, compounding pharmacies, and death penalty abolition activism play out quite spectacularly through the "accidents" affecting bodies executed by lethal injection. Failed executions demonstrate how the effects of the chemonorms generated by this interplay of politics with chemical agency are unequally distributed, and bodies on death row are forced to carry the brunt of these toxic burdens. From this, it is possible to see how trans-corporeality contests abstract and universal accounts of subjectivity and demonstrates how some bodies are made more vulnerable by systemic forces. Once we acknowledge these multiscalar entanglements between bodies and their habitats, it becomes impossible to think of environmental issues as "external" problems that have no bearing on exercises of punitive power.

Pathological Normativity

Across the previous four chapters, I have explored the possibilities of nonhuman normativity, examined how environmental forces shape the development of human law, and outlined why this is significant for the sociolegal study of punishment. For Davies, nature's propensity to shape social norms and human law reveals a fresh and different way of theorising natural law, as the immanent normativity that comes with living alongside and through a Nature that produces its own values and enacts its own norms. Within the *nomos*, "human beings are both subject and object in different normative worlds".[24]

As Davies explains, when we create norms to protect nature or prevent the destruction of the environment, we focus on norms created by the "human side" and for "human ends". Western thinking has historically been dominated by this kind of paternalism towards any group that has been defined as other – living and non-living. Consequently, our environmental norms and rules are based on the presumption that nature is incapable of protecting itself. In the face of a vulnerable and passive nature, there is no alternative for humans *but* to step in.[25] However, throughout this book, I have drawn attention to the ways in which Nature resists human activity and resets human paths.

It is impossible to appreciate nature's agency, its capacity to affect and be affected, when changes in its patterns of behaviour are written off as anomalies and mishaps. In the introduction to "Nonorganic Life", Manuel de Landa explains how our ideas and ways of looking at the world may prevent us from discerning the presence and significance of phenomena. He explains how, for instance, "Western astronomers were 'unable' to see changes in the cosmos…Sunspots, for example, remained 'invisible' – that is, insignificant and anomalous – *until* Copernicus' ideas changed the ways in which European astronomers could look at the heavens".[26] Without these paradigm shifts, many of the phenomena we notice but cannot explain using our existing knowledge practices are too easily dismissed as insignificant accidents.

Using Canguilhem's work, Davies refers to these sudden shifts in nature's normal patterns of behaviour as "pathological": "[p]athology is not just difference from a prior state of normality but exists where a diversion from the norm is resisted by organisms".[27] Pathologies challenge vital normativity, normative behaviours that preserve life. Yet, "an anomaly experienced by an organism is not of itself pathological because it might be functional or adaptive: it might be useful".[28] The spherulation of Cocci is but one example of the pathological, adaptive processes that emerged out of a necessity to survive in human and animal ecologies. Over time, alongside environment, what was once pathological became normalised. As Davies remarks, "'normality' is a quality of neither the organism nor the environment but of both together".[29]

24 Davies, *EcoLaw* , 2.

25 Davies (n 24) 2.

26 Manuel De Landa, 'Nonorganic Life' in Jonathan Crary and Sanford Kwinter (eds), *Incorporations* (MIT Press 1992) 129.

27 Davies (n 24) 59.

28 Ibid.

29 Ibid., 60.

Nothing in the world is "chance", "the environment's inconstancy is simply its becoming, its history".[30]

Davies conceptualises vital normativity differently than Canguilhem. While he sees it as "something that attaches to organisms", she describes it as "arising within the complexities of ecosystems".[31] Vital norms are produced out of the need for life to continue in a particular way. Similarly, *social norms*, too, are immanent with "needs and purposes that are the product of geographical and historical-cultural circumstances".[32] But as Davies notes, human societies live by way of not only social norms but also intentionally designed rule systems in the form of state law and regulation; "society is both machine and organism".[33] Within such a framing, the pathological becomes a normative judgement made by sociolegal systems. Pathologies – disease and botched executions – arise from the system's failure to adapt, to engage ethically and materially with the ecological world. Pathologies arise from structural flaws such as anthropocentrism, dualism, colonialism, racism, technocentrism, and capitalism embedded in a system destructively misaligned with ecological realities.

Applying Davies' insights to the failed execution or disease epidemics can allow us to see these events not just as failures of technical procedure or risk management, but as revelatory ruptures that expose the plastic and unstable nature of state violence and political subjectivity, the norms and processes by which humans live. The pathologies of disease and spectacular death recast the state's exercise of violence as clumsy and barbaric and transform the condemned from a perpetrator of suffering to a suffering victim. While the legal system designed both incarceration and execution as a swift, clean, peaceful closure to the violent, chaotic, impulsive acts of those it condemned, these "pathologies" reveal the state's own violence, the fragility of its own forms of control. Pathologies are not just interruptions of justice. They trigger debates about what justice through violence becomes. The normative power of the pathological lies in its ability to signal the presence of hazard in what appears mundane. By tracing the microbial and chemical patterns of intra-action that give rise to pathological events, I have sought to bring to light the ever-presence of exposure and risk, even in the absence of spectacular deaths and disease. Thinking about the pathological as normative helps move us away from the romantic and orderly view of nature that has long underscored western philosophy, and which does not conceive of rupture, disfiguration, unpredictability as productive forces, as events and becomings that trigger both material and social change. Yet, this capacity for transformation is a key

30 Ibid.
31 Ibid., 61.
32 Ibid.
33 Ibid.

attribute of failed executions and disease epidemics in prisons, as events and becomings that spark emotional upset, generate political debate, and provoke legal challenge. Pathological events are affective; they move us in ways that are more visceral than rational. In so doing, the pathological provokes a turn to the body – to affect and emotion as measures of the ethical.

Punishing in the Anthropocene

In writing this book, I have sought to challenge the dominant view that punishment is an intimate affair between the state and its law-breakers. In particular, I have tried to expose how questions about marginalisation, social inequality, and social disadvantage come to bear on the experience of punishment through *material* channels that remain unexplored within dominant sociolegal accounts. There is no dearth of research which examines the sociopolitical sources of inequality, marginalisation and disadvantage and how these shape individual experiences of punishment. I consider some of this scholarship in Chapter 1 of this book. Nevertheless, I believe there are also a whole range of ecological sources that remain unacknowledged, typically on account of our enduring belief in human exceptionalism and transcendentalism, all of which create an image of the nonhuman world as not only distinct and separate from the social world, but also a place characterised by mechanical passivity. Journeying through Chapters 2, 3, and 4, I hope you will agree that this is a mischaracterisation of the world we write off as "nature". To the extent that humans are material beings, porous bodies, composed of multiple and shifting chemo/geo/hydro/microbial-ecologies, the nonhuman world is always *part* of us, and our activities leave a tangible imprint on the world we inhabit. These intra-actions, as Chapter 3 and 4 demonstrated, have a bearing on how, where, and whom we punish. As Nick Fox explains "recognising that humans assemble with a range of nonhuman matter allows us to open up new questions and find new answers".[34]

This book has never been about finding the "causes" of what makes incarceration or the death penalty cruel and unusual. If anything, I believe this book has sought to uncover the ways in which our understanding of cruel and unusual punishment is unjustifiably narrow, perhaps *because* it seeks causes; how it unfairly limits ethical questions to individual intent and institutional action; how it oversimplifies and reduces complex phenomena to simple cause-and-effect analyses and how, in doing so, it treats everything that is not human – geological and hydrological forces, climate, microbes, chemicals – as stable and inattentive, and thus irrelevant to the law. As a consequence of

34 Anna Grear and others, '"Acting Amidst" – A Conversation with Jane Bennett, Facilitated by Anna Grear' (2025) 16 Journal of Human Rights and the Environment 46, 46.

this neglect, we lose sight of how local phenomena are a confluence of the political economies of near and far, past and present, and how we humans are deeply entangled with its emergence. Our bodies are "hyperlocal"[35] frames of multiscalar activity such that "even as we scale inward to [the] body's most mundane functions, by proxy we [are] also scaling outward to talk about" the sociopolitical contexts through which the body is materially constituted.[36] These are entanglements that we may not be aware of, entanglements that may produce consequences that we may not even recognise as significant until much later in the future, entanglements that we have never consented to, and most importantly, entanglements that are differently experienced across human society. .

Taken together, the chapters of *Punishment* highlight experiences of environmental injustice within penal systems, showing how such harms are produced not only be social actors but also by ecological processes, how they are lived by those who are incarcerated or executed, and how they resonate with the rest of us. We can view constitutional challenges about prisoners contracting Valley Fever as isolated exposures to toxic environments, or we can understand them as part of a wider material and ideological system that creates such conditions and systematically places those deemed undesirable in their path. Similarly, we can view executions that do not go to plan as mere instances of human error, or we can see them as part of broader systems of knowledge that frame nature as lifeless, operate through global capital and transnational corporations, and assume human mastery over a nature that exists for our exploitation. In the first instance, envisioning Nature as indifferent and mechanical is likely to produce feelings of despair, the idea that Nature is inescapably cruel. In the second, imagining nature as submissive or malleable to human interest generates a false sense of security, the idea that Nature has calculable meaning, and all that is needed is for us to figure out this inner logic. In both instances, we become disenchanted by a Nature that seems relentlessly indifferent.[37]

It would be amiss to think that a desire for political or legal intervention is the primary aim of *Punishment*. It may be more appropriate here to imagine its aim as, in Bennett's words, encouraging "endeavours whose efficacy is better described as *inflection* or *influence*", the promotion of practices that are directed at figuring out "how stuff happens".[38] As she notes, there is some-

35 See Theresa Dillon's contribution in Ibid., 48.

36 Vanessa Agard-Jones, 'Bodies in the System' (2013) 17 Small Axe 182, 183.

37 Max Weber, 'Gesammlte Aufsaetze Zur Wissenschaftslehre (Science as Vocation)' (Duncker & Humboldt, Munich 1919) <https://www.wisdom.weizmann.ac.il/~oded/X/WeberScienceVocation.pdf> accessed 11 September 2021. I have also applied Weber's concept of *Entzauberung* to the death penalty, see Sabrina Gilani, 'The Ethics of Capital Punishment and a Law of Affective Enchantment' (2023) 32 Social & Legal Studies 3.

38 Grear and others (n 35) 47.

thing of value in acquainting oneself to the "subtle feel for the process in play, a feel that would make possible action 'upstream' from effects".[39] Pragmatic change follows on from, I believe, alterations in how one *feels* events, actions, phenomena, as an "affective buzz".[40]

To some extent then, my ecological view of punishment calls for a "re-embodiment" of legal subjectivity, an attunement to the sensing (and sense-able), affected (and affecting) body as it encounters "alternative imagined configurations which can be recognised as making both cognitive *and* affective sense".[41] As Grear explains, "[c]entral to law's imaginary, in the liberal legal tradition, is the potent founding of a fiction of the liberal social contract, folded into the foundations of which is a highly particular [propertied] subject" bearing an "imaginary embodiment [that is] complexly disembodied".[42] This erects a "rational" legal subject, "for whom/which everything else (including the human body itself) functions as 'object'".[43] It is her contention that this abstract, detached, rational subject of the law is an imaginary that both reflects and perpetuates colonial oppression and neocolonial violence, ecological destruction and capitalist exploitation. She envisions this new "re-embodiment" as deeply posthuman, in the sense of materially entangled and productive of, what she calls, "sympoietic normativities", norms generated through mutual co-dependence and co-emergence between the human-more-than-human world.[44] This kind of reworlding of law would attribute significance to nonhuman agency by treating corporeality and affective encounters as ethical matters, worthy of legal attention while simultaneously reaching out to epistemic framings that have been largely ignored by western bodies of knowledge, including the arts, ecology, mathematics, and sciences.[45]

While I subtitled this chapter "Posthuman Punishment", I am acutely aware of the ideological baggage that the term carries. Not all of the thinkers I have discussed over the course of this book embrace the term "the posthuman". Even some of those who have been largely responsible for popularising posthumanism, such as Donna Haraway and Cary Wolfe, remain sceptical of its use.[46] "Posthumanism" has been criticised for lacking conceptual

39 Ibid.

40 See Bennett's contribution in Ibid., 51.

41 Here Grear is citing Lennon's work. *See*, Anna Grear, 'Legal Imaginaries and the Anthropocene: "Of" and "For"' (2020) 31 Law and Critique 351, 351.

42 Ibid., 352.

43 Ibid.

44 Ibid., 361.

45 Haraway (n 3) 70–98.

46 Donna J Haraway, *When Species Meet* (University of Minnesota Press 2008) 17; Cary Wolfe, *What Is Posthumanism?*, vol. 8 (University of Minnesota Press 2010) xv; Alison Ravenscroft, 'Strange Weather: Indigenous Materialisms, New Materialism, and Colonialism' (2018) 5 Cambridge Journal of Postcolonial Literary Inquiry 353; Manuel De Landa, *Assemblage Theory* (Edinburgh University Press 2016).

clarity,[47] ignoring the question of social inequality,[48] being overly celebratory of technology,[49] and overlooking important politico-ethical considerations.[50] At the same time, I do think it is possible to embrace a posthuman methodology (as many of these authors do), while still remaining cognisant of its many trappings. I use the term "posthuman" to encourage a reworlding of punishment theory, practice, and discourse to account for sources, effects, and relationalities that include more than *just* humans, but also include humans in a way that most sociolegal theorists have never thought about them before – as porous, entangled, co-becoming subjectivities. Humans – using Frost's terminology – as "biocultural creatures".[51] To that end, this book has sought to draw attention to the entanglements between punishment ethics, political economy, and global and planetary flows of matter, and is firmly rooted in the view that the three cannot be separated because "even the smallest, most personal ethical practices in the domestic sphere are inextricably tied to any number of massive political and economic predicaments, such as global capitalism, labour and class injustice, climate injustice, neoliberalism, neocolonialism, industrial agriculture, factory farming, pollution, climate change, and extinction".[52]

Mainstream punishment discourse must reimagine what it means to punish ethically in a world where harmful experiences of punishment cannot be attributed to individual human cruelty alone. The posthuman lens adopted in this book brings these failures into focus by centring chemical and microbial agency. The lethal injection does not simply "deliver" death according to human design; its chemical contents are capable of behaviours and affective intensities that may run afoul of the quiet, serene, precise death that the state desires and which the courts require as justification for the death penalty. Similarly, questions about how we punish acceptably also become complicated in the face of new discoveries that show that our forms of punishment can have effects that ripple across generations, affecting the health and well-being of individuals who have never been convicted of criminal wrongdoing. How do we take responsibility for failures in punitive power – executions that go awry, fungal infections that become deadly – in a world where the sources and effects of these failures can be traced to events far away and histories long ago? How far do we go to trace their emergence? Or do we let go of our obsession with identifying causes as an essential element of attributing responsibility and rethink responsibility as prospective; responsibility as

47 De Landa (n 47); Karen Barad, *Meeting the Universe Halfway: Quantum Physics and the Entanglement of Matter and Meaning* (Duke University Press 2007).

48 Chen (n 12).

49 Wolfe (n 47).

50 De Landa (n 27); Alaimo (n 22).

51 Samantha Frost, 'Biocultural Creatures', *Biocultural Creatures* (Duke University Press 2016).

52 Alaimo (n 11) 10–11.

a duty or obligation to mitigate effects? It is my hope that *Punishment* has, if nothing else, convinced you that how we think about and practise punishment must be more attentive to Nature, for, in the Anthropocene, we live as precarious creatures, endeavouring to shape Nature to our whims while remaining materially entangled in its attentive and resistive becomings.

Works Cited

Agard-Jones V, 'Bodies in the System' (2013) 17 Small Axe 182.

Alaimo S, *Bodily Natures: Science, Environment, and the Material Self* (Indiana University Press 2010).

Alaimo S, *Exposed* (University of Minnesota Press 2016).

Barad K, *Meeting the Universe Halfway: Quantum Physics and the Entanglement of Matter and Meaning* (Duke University Press 2007).

Barad K, 'Troubling Time/s and Ecologies of Nothingness: Re-Turning, Re-Membering, and Facing the Incalculable' (2018) 92 New Formations: A Journal of Culture/Theory/Politics 56.

Chen MY, *Intoxicated: Race, Disbaility and Chemical Intimacy Across Empire* (Duke University Press 2023).

Cutter SL, 'Race, Class and Environmental Justice' (1995) 19 Progress in Human Geography 111.

Davies M, *EcoLaw: Legality, Life, and the Normativity of Nature* (Taylor & Francis 2022).

De Landa M, *Assemblage Theory* (Edinburgh University Press 2016).

De Landa M, 'Nonorganic Life' in Jonathan Crary and Sanford Kwinter (eds), *Incorporations* (MIT Press 1992).

Foster S, 'Race(Ial)Matters: The Quest for Environmental Justice' (1993) 20 Ecology Law Quarterly 721.

Frost S, *Biocultural Creatures* (Duke University Press 2016).

Gilani S, 'The Ethics of Capital Punishment and a Law of Affective Enchantment' (2023) 32 Social & Legal Studies 3.

Grear A, '"Acting Amidst" – A Conversation with Jane Bennett, Facilitated by Anna Grear' (2025) 16 Journal of Human Rights and the Environment 46.

Grear A, 'Legal Imaginaries and the Anthropocene: "Of" and "For"' (2020) 31 Law and Critique 351.

Haraway D, *Staying with the Trouble: Making Kin in the Chthulucene* (Duke University Press 2016).

Haraway DJ, *When Species Meet* (University of Minnesota Press 2008).

Kirk G, 'Ecofeminism and Environmental Justice: Bridges across Gender, Race, and Class' (1997) 18 Frontiers: A Journal of Women Studies 2.

Kuznetski (Nee Tofantsuk JK (née and Alaimo S, 'Transcorporeality: An Interview with Stacy Alaimo' (2020) 11 Ecozon@: European Journal of Literature, Culture and Environment 137.

Lewis D and others, 'Linking Land Displacement and Environmental Dispossession to Mi'kmaw Health and Well-Being: Culturally Relevant Place-Based Interpretive Frameworks Matter' (2021) 65 Canadian Geographies / Géographies canadiennes 66.

Moore JW, *Anthropocene or Capitalocene?: Nature, History, and the Crisis of Capitalism* (PM Press 2016).

Murphy M, *Sick Building Syndrome and the Problem of Uncertainty: Environmental Politics, Technoscience, and Women Workers* (Duke University Press 2006).

Nixon R, *Slow Violence and the Environmentalism of the Poor* (Harvard University Press 2011).

Papadopoulos D, 'Chemicals, Ecology, and Reparative Justice' in Dimitris Papadopoulos, Maria Puig de la Bellacasa and Natasha Myers (eds), *Reactivating Elements: Chemistry, Ecology, Practice* (Duke University Press 2021).

Ravenscroft A, 'Strange Weather: Indigenous Materialisms, New Materialism, and Colonialism' (2018) 5 Cambridge Journal of Postcolonial Literary Inquiry 353.

Shapiro N, 'Attuning to the Chemosphere: Domestic Formaldehyde, Bodily Reasoning, and the Chemical Sublime' (2015) 30 Cultural Anthropology 368.

Stewart K, 'Atmospheric Attunements' (2011) 29 Environment and Planning D: Society and Space 445.

Tsing A, 'Contaminated Diversity in "Slow Disturbance": Potential Collaborators for a Liveable Earth' in Gary Martin, Diana Mincyte and Ursula Münster (eds), *Why Do We Value Diversity? Biocultural Diversity in a Global Context* (RCC Perspectives 2012), 95–98.

Weber M, 'Gesammlte Aufsaetze Zur Wissenschaftslehre (Science as Vocation)' (Duncker & Humboldt, Munich 1919) <https://www.wisdom.weizmann.ac.il/~oded/X/WeberScienceVocation.pdf> accessed 11 September 2021.

Wolfe C, *What Is Posthumanism?*, vol. 8 (University of Minnesota Press 2010).

Index

For Product Safety Concerns and Information please contact our EU representative GPSR@taylorandfrancis.com Taylor & Francis Verlag GmbH, Kaufingerstraße 24, 80331 München, Germany

Printed and bound by CPI Group (UK) Ltd, Croydon, CR0 4YY
14/09/2026
02216223-0008